MW01260112

My Mother's Red Ford

# MY MOTHER'S RED FORD

*New & Selected Poems* · 1986 - 2020

## Roy Bentley

LOST HORSE PRESS
Sandpoint, Idaho

*Author Photo:* Original World Enterprises.
*Book Design:* Christine Lysnewycz Holbert.

FIRST EDITION

This and other award-winning LOST HORSE PRESS titles may be viewed on our website at www.losthorsepress.org.

LIBRARY OF CONGRESS CATALOGING-IN-PUBLICATION DATA

Cataloguing-in-Publication Data may be obtained from the Library of Congress.

# Contents

## V

## *from* **Walking with Eve in the Loved City (2018)**

# VI

## *from* **Body of a Deer by a Creek in Summer (2018)**

## VII

## New Poems

*for Lee Martin*

# from Boy in a Boat

## 1953

### 1

In Fleming, Kentucky, the hills rise up.
Walking the ridge, gathering blackberries,
she hears a rasp of crickets, yap of dogs
chasing children in the dust.
Down the hollow near where she lives
wet horses walk through shoulder-high corn,
leaves parting to let them pass.

### 2

Back from Ashland Pen her husband has his
picture taken on the fender of a '46 Chevy truck;
sees on the sidewalk in front of the drugstore
Junior Tucker who helped sell the whiskey
that got him a year. As if it would buy it all back,
he catches Tuck with one good right, then a left.

There is nothing hurried in the way he says it—
"That son-of-a-bitch shot me"—
and walks the block or so to Fleming Hospital.
There, quiet, kidding with a nurse he'd
gone to school with,
hole in his liver the size of a dime:
*Go tell Mary.*

### 3

"Live long enough and you bury 'em all," she says,
staring at the 8 x 10, thin man
leaning forward into gray.
All those years, his children,
tying first shoes,
to bury him on the hill above Goose Creek
in the rain—

casket into flat bed, road straight up,
slipping in clay, catching herself,
truck chain stretched tight, holding this once.

## Christmas, Coffman's Farm

North corner of the near field,
abandoned grain barn, Ford tractor on blocks.
Nearer the house by a cistern, three
snowmen it took ladders to finish,
biggest with a smile half its face.
Across the yard, in porchlight,

cats claw each other for a half-plate of chicken,
snow flying the few minutes it takes
the big Gray to win out.
Year-old child presses against door glass,
claps his hands. In the kitchen
his mother to a man next to her:
"Told you they's hungry."

Last of the sun warm on the door
cat comes quiet to the porch, raises itself
even with the child. At the glass small mouths open.
Steam catches the sound.

## Night Fishing the Ohio

He knows something, this old shovelhead.
Close in, like good whiskey,
he has the blood believing again.
Yet a part of him needs the hook,
its pull into light, to keep going.
The Masonic Lodge of Belpre, Ohio, would agree.
On the near bank, two of their number
brace a weight of wood and oxbone,
carry it stumbling, sidestepping an old dog.

In a clearing by lantern light,
every full belly recalls the flesh,
takes its turn, hefts ax and sledge,
breaks the ribs, spine,
legs stripped now of all that muscle.
I feel each hard blow ring
at the bait-end of 12-pound test.
Bone bits spray outward in the dark.
Upstream, deer lean across and into barbed wire,
the apples there worth a little blood.

## White Handkerchief

*And did you see the handkerchief?*

—Iago: *Othello*, Act IV, scene 1

### 1

The first time I had my fortune told
was by a woman who taught English
at a technical school.
Had a black belt in judo.
*Pick a card*, she said and played a tape
of Peter, Paul and Mary.

I pointed to the King of Cups.
*Cut them*, she said.
How much I believed of what she said
is hard to say.
In a way, I believed it all.
When she was finished,
I gave her a ride into Nelsonville, dropped her
at a Sohio station as if magic belonged there.
She drove away in a Jeep.

### 2

On a small rise the third week of spring,
walking,
I notice at the edge of a leaf in wind
a moment in which the underside
can be seen clearly, when rise and fall
are one motion, connection tenuous as rain.

Legs are stiff with going up.
I see that turning repeated, recall the night
Tom Kozlowski spoke in tongues
in a basement in Newark, Ohio.
Tom rocking, chanting,

I heard what I took to be God,
afterwards, asked how much was his.
Shrugging, Tom smiled: *You tell me.*

3

When I was thirteen, Virgil Horsley
stood at the front of the Heath Baptist Church,
white handkerchief in his cupped hand,
and in the lightest Southern accent I have ever heard
told me I was lost. My grandmother
who read to me from a big King James—
"and the blood came trickling down"—
would have been proud as I went forward,
tears streaming
all the way to nineteen when I cut my wrist
and saw bright and gray in the meat
how stupid it would be to waste this.

Now, in the middle distance,
I hear Virgil Horsley too is lost—
shipped out on a tanker, drunk,
ranting there is no God.
Suddenly the weather changes
and he is part of whatever it means
to say something is past protecting.

On dry land it is easy to separate out
the brick church by Ramp Creek, dull voice
that pleaded its way through 1967:
*One more verse. While we wait.*

## Why Mark Chapman Got Both Legs of His Good Pants Wet

It was 1970, my first poem,
and I read in a high-school restroom, Mark Chapman
laughing so hard he fell, cussing,
into a half-wall urinal.
The handful who gathered to help him up
marveled either at the power of the spoken word
or the spectacle. After, in biology,
boat-shaped mitochondria steered blind,
lanky chromosomes bent like fishermen
leaning into more than they could land.

On the Tennessee River that year
we fished with ropes the warmer water
below TVA dams,
whole small bluegill as bait,
bank-end of the rope staked deep
because a 40-pound catfish tears arms free
if it hits right.
What hook and rope accomplished below the dams,
I wanted done in that restroom.
Never mind that mad, high laugh
as if what I was doing was slapstick,
Fields or Chaplin. It was a dark year.
The clear things were fish and dividing cells—
furrows in cytoplasm stained visible and dead,
shovelhead big and slick as the floor
that met Mark Chapman.

The last class of the day was history.
Had it been 1770, men like Simon Kenton—
six days naked in winter, Shawnee
near enough to touch—
I might have written of a land called *Can-tuc-kee*,
game plentiful and God so present
he rated two names.

Might have written of the gauntlet,
Shawnee method of testing courage: two lines,
club and tomahawk blows on a common lane.
The trick then was not to stop, to shout
either of God's names and run with every cell
straining to light. Almost no one made it.
You knew that when you ran.

## In Praise of That Same Motion

The night Ed Laurienzo ran a kickoff back 87 yards,
slipping six tackles, I sat beside
Sandy Langford at Newark High Stadium.
Eddie was so smooth, falling
forward the last few feet to score.
And after the game,
backseat of my mother's Ford,
stretched out, windows steamed from our breath,
we came so close.
At the last minute she sat up, wiped a window
to see out.

Years later, in her backyard,
I remember her telling me not to marry.
There, in the heat of summer, August,
I told her I wouldn't. Then,
calling up names of men she liked as well,
sent her an invitation, next day in the mail.

There is a part of us that longs to move
like Eddie Laurienzo, ever forward,
freeing ourselves. And if we can dream but once
we have the ball, game dead even,
see a hole the size of Cleveland, and falling,
spinning, finding the mark
make it 22-16, why not?

*On the Diamond Behind Garfield Elementary,*
*Melvin White Proves There Is But One Boog Powell*

When Dave Wheeler fielded the hard one-hopper
to short, he fired the ball to Melvin White,
forgetting the huge first baseman
moved like molasses.
Melvin caught it on his sternum.
You could hear the breath escaping
all the way to center field.

Falling in love is like that,
begging air as the infield laughs hysterically.
You could be dying, blue and big as Melvin White.
It could be spring and the woman married.
She could be dark
and fine as air the hour after rain.
Still, they would double over laughing,
the pain getting worse.

And after she had gone,
you would catch her scent, imagine
strong small hands halving apricots
as you fall face first, runner advancing.
Of course, eventually the pain would ease.
You would stand.
It would be important that the game go on.
You would recall a score,
how far behind you were when it hit,
only this bright burning in the lungs.

## The Young American Wrestles His First Harley-Davidson

*for Billy Barnett*

"Clutch stuck," you told us
and pushed the black '48 panhead
up the embankment. Mounted again.
Rode with a curse for God on your lips.
Same curse set free at fifteen:
stealing the tin roof to Frances Potter's barn,
selling the metal. Five dollars, a month of Marlboros.

What was it about you nothing could conquer?
the good looks? the way you shot straight pool?
the time you put a diamondback in the glove box
of your truck, made Dolores (your sister)
listen to the rattle and hiss
the four and three-quarter miles
down Pound Mountain? Try anything once.

Today, it is 1961. June.
The foot clutch has slipped, and you smile
as the big bike hook-slides you and it
under my father's truck.
A last red-lettered flash: *Roy's Shell. AX8-9381.*
Tall, thin Ronnie Hall laughing, choking hard
on a Coca-Cola.

Eight years and you will lean over a shotgun.
Send that James Dean myth and one blue eye
into the wall.
This minute though, Billy, you're a hero.
A minor god I trade shirts with.

## Shirts

The shirt I slept in is wrinkled now. It lies beside
my bed, quiet—a squirrel I buried one Christmas.
Both sleeves, still rolled, cross like pages of the paper
we used as shroud. The shirt is brown. I have
seven the same: I am reminding myself that each day

is a dream I wear, walk in
till something strips me. It is hard to dream.

Six shirts hang in the closet. The one she bought
that Christmas, lost; one among many
I may have worn it
today. I cannot know. Six sets of arms stand as one
in shadow, edges smoothed in. I count them.
Tomorrow and tomorrow are as these—the seventh
spreading itself: an animal almost still.

There is a darkness here, one I am familiar with.
Yet it comes inside as if it were the first time: slowly,
watching the eyes. I entered a woman once like this—
at Christmas, her parents shopping. Hearing them
in the garage we hurried upstairs; saw her father
with the small body—the squirrel—holding it,

stroking cold. It was a gift from a previous summer.
I recall how she stood naming it, cradling newspaper
until I took it away, the cheap gray staying.

I am reminded by all things of that which is left.
By fragments and by feel I piece it back.
It is this hard to dream. After sleep I rise,
dress in brown, sleeves surrounding me.
It is a good fit.

## Barracks

### 1

When they brought Jack Parrish back the third time
he had tears in his eyes, both wrists bandaged
where the metal of the cuffs had dug in.
He dropped down heavy on the bed,
rubbed his arm, recalling
how they dragged him kicking, from the waterfront,
beat him three flights up from the hold of a ship.
I offer him a cigarette.
"Had it made," he says, pack-tapping it tight.
I sit, taking it in,
hearing Jack inhale, breathe out,
smoke rising, thinning
like the sound a mattress makes,
springs yielding to the weight of this or any man.

### 2

The room I share with him is small.
The door, left open, leaves it seeming larger.
"Fuck This Shit" is carved in the wall above my bed.
I lie on my back, reading the last thirty years,
fall asleep, still in uniform,
and Jack, entering, wakes me.

He does not mention last winter when I slit my wrist,
circled, in blood, the words on the wall,
says nothing of his father's suicide.
He has a new girl, comes in dancing,
naked to the waist, singing Sinatra.
That night as we lie talking,
he tells me he is afraid for his mother,
being beaten by a man she is afraid to leave.
"I try to have faith," he says. "I pray."

In a week he would strangle on his own vomit,
the only casualty of a party in Parrish Hall—
I swear to God.

3

A year after Parrish I am out.
The day I sign the papers the sun is shining.
Five hours later, bus leaving Rantoul,
it begins to rain.
A girl in the street waves to me
from under her umbrella. In Columbus,
a cab driver shatters that, tries to make me.
4 a.m., High Street in the rain, I almost let him.
Then I remember the words above my bed,
get out at the light.

## Arcana

*A divine nimbus exhales from it*
*from head to foot . . .*
*Hair, bosom, hips, bend of legs,*
*negligent falling hands all diffused.*

—Walt Whitman

The spring Butch Thompson and I rented a trailer
in Rantoul, Illinois, the sun rose each morning
through a diamond-shaped window on the wood door.
Within a week of moving in, Butch had covered
the diamond with a poster of Tina Turner.
First light began between her thighs.
I never want to forget that.

I move tonight in borrowed clothes, my uncle's,
his good scent flown with any clear memory of him.
Four years after his death
I can muster only that ecstatic look
at a discussion of freemasonry, every handshake
and shibboleth gone up like kindling.
In the stove, dry-stacked maple and birch bark,
striate and smooth, burns and down.
Changed air hurries against the cold.

It is a poor soldiery marks our going,
and little calls us back.
Consider the night Walt Whitman met
with Secretary of the Treasury Salmon P. Chase,
Republican from Ohio, to discuss a possible clerkship.
Consider how Whitman held in his hand
a signed letter from Ralph Waldo Emerson;
how Salmon P. Chase did not sing the body electric;
how the Secretary of the Treasury dreamed
of the Presidency after Lincoln; how he collected
signatures. Consider Whitman speaking eloquently

of the Union dead, of the necessity of not forgetting,
while Chase mentally positioned the framed Emerson
on the wall between Longfellow and Francis Scott Key.

Consider Butch Thompson, sunrise
on South Chanute Street,
all that blazing symmetry and a brand new day.

## Upon Trying the Door of Mark Twain's House

### 1

At 17, the road to Hannibal, Missouri,
is hours of corn- and beanfield—
honeysuckled barnsides,
clear May sky the only limit.
Three days a runaway, I stand finally
before the white two-story, corner drainspout
smooth with down-sliding at midnight.
"After five," a caretaker apologizes,
leaves me to look in lower floor windows.

When I have seen enough—Hill Street
and the famous fence, tea roses in bloom—
I walk to Becky Thatcher's Bookstore,
steal a copy of *Life on the Mississippi*.
Outside, beyond Mark Twain Savings & Loan,
noise of men drunk as boys, side-arming stones
into water part Wapsipinicon, part the Des Moines.

### 2

My uncle, William Barnett, wears a hat like Bogart:
big-brimmed, the kind that hides thinning hair.
This morning he buries a brother-in-law.
Outside Banks and Craft Funeral Home, under eaves
as rain pours down,
I want him to tell me about the time
he went for a loaf of bread, joined the Navy.
How it was he neglected to tell them
he had four children, a wife; later,
how he got Blanche to see the recruiter.
*Lady, don't you s'pose he knew he had them kids?*
In the haze of this played-out town
he says only, "Gonna be a bitch, that hill.
Was with Earl." As always the dread comes first—

twenty years, mornings going from light
into the close dark of mines
that cross Whitesburg, Fleming-Neon even now.
First the dread, then God only knows.
We do well not to send him after bread.

## The L & K Plays Host to the Class of '72

In a restaurant off Hebron Road,
between the Sohio and Doc Gutridge's place,
we drank Cokes one summer and talked to death
the few dreams Heath, Ohio had its hands on.
*Rod Sloneker, Jerry Peters.* We would pull in.
*Mike Yoder, Ed Laurienzo.* Seven, seven-thirty.
*Don Surratt, Mark Chapman.* And order and talk
till they locked the doors around ten.
*Dave Hanley, Tom Kozlowski.*
Ice water and air-conditioning
that June, July, and August.
I remember most the air at night, still hot,
smell from the one refinery and how it
nudged us sleepers in our places there
between Ramp Creek and the Licking River.
Even the dogs at Doc Gutridge's wanted to wake us.
The song that year was "Anticipation." A8.
Pushed till the buttons stayed.
In the parking lot, on Mark Chapman's Ford,
we counted change—
how many quarts of three-two beer
we had between us. Into the light came Camaros.
*Jo Anne Clutter, April Fisher.* Idling, numinous.
*Diane Harkness, Sherri Link.* Wide-eyed.
*Beth McDonald, Bettie Seaman, Robin White.*
Bright as every wish that fell from fenders,
from three-inch speakers, the same one song.

# II

*from* **Any One Man**

## The Country of the Dead

*The vast country of the dead*
*had its beginning everywhere . . .*

—Czeslaw Milosz

We sit in the paneled basement
of his house in Ohio and listen
to a doctor in Sao Paulo sputter,
in perfect English, about ionic skip,
waves of voice at the speed of light
bounced, with little loss, day to night

to day. The room is radios and coaxial cable
at arm's length. A dark Zenith Trans-Oceanic
he listened to the year I was born
collects dust forlornly on a parts shelf.
*Honolulu,* he says, *is nothing—*
biweekly, talks weather, rain or dry,

with Melbourne, Australia.
When I was a boy, 17,
Led Zeppelin albums spun between these walls.
Other atmospheres of marijuana smoke
circled up and out through opened window wells.
Everything familiar

was made over years ago, remodeled
and sealed to soundproof,
antennae tower outside, above—
where I scratched names, a heart, *Love Forever—*
superseded, sold for scrap.
The handful of women who undressed

and let go mysteries below my parents' bed
would never admit to so much of us

so scrupulously lost, one memory
like another like something else or nothing
very much must have happened here.
I want to ask the doctor in Brazil

what my father would think foolish:
whether random connecting like this,
continent to continent,
ever goes beyond words and megahertz—
*Talking air,* my mother calls it.
I think of silence as message, whistling engine:

the bounty and emptiness,
measured, looping adventure of electricity
bound in that lightning-becomes-voice instant
of science and sense, all of it burning.
If there were call letters, a frequency
for the condition of hearts,

signal would diminish in transit, an answer
begin, Say again. The doctor
speaks of the necessary death
of rain forest to the north, of exports
and topless beaches. Says the trick
is to look and not look.

## Giants

Martin and Anna Bates, new-married, ease legs-first
to the feather-bedded floor of a wagon. Martin,
seven foot six and a half inches, in Anna's big arms,
pictures crews of Irish and Welsh felling miles of two-span
beech poplar maple, whole ancient-timbered sections
of Letcher County, Kentucky. Anna, seven foot five inches,
beside him, pregnant, has asked he not mention going home.
She too remembers, says the circus is food and a future
for two so accustomed to stares. He opens the twelve-pound
pocket watch, wrought gold gift of Victoria,
Queen of Great Britain, Empress of India.
In the still night on Hampshire Downs, Martin Bates,
sideshow attraction, hears a mill wheel turn and take water.

•

Rain pops for hours on the canvas, lakes of it leveed
and exploding levees. Near morning, after making love,
Martin remarks how his son or daughter should know
the simple ring and return of fiddle music,
how joy, like a whiskey, begins at a boil in the mountains.

•

There are ways there and back
the trigonometries of which resolve quietly, luminously,
into the ability to bear the weight of the going.
Ships in open sea, in approaching storm,
intuit angels of ice and wind and spoiling wave,
courses put across at precisely the moment
when what is summonable is outline and foreign.
Mid-ocean, cupped hands of companionable light resist charting.
The trusted sextant sights and resights,
being all the equipment of habit that works.

And what of firm soil after undulating months at sea,
landed horizonline so finite and abruptly vertical
as to make of the slow extendings of continents
something dreamed? The world ashore censed
with high lapping, bay breezes that track and sweep us,
spilling news of essential things: cramped trains
of immigrant and native crossing insular slopes,
level miles of trestled valley. In one lighted traincar,
a man takes the gloved hands of a large woman, uncovers
and kisses them, equally.

◆

In a log house by the thawing north fork of the Kentucky River,
Anna Bates has just pushed out the largest live birth
in recorded history. Twenty-three pounds eleven ounces.
Bruised, it breathes and follows Martin's watch.
When it dies near evening, unnamed, Anna will kiss
and wrap a brooding likeness, famous body purchased by wire
by a health museum in Cleveland, Ohio;
where, in a white room, behind glass, suspended,
it is the shadowed face of Elkhorn Creek, Pound Gap,
the Cumberlands. *Look at me,* it says. *For one day,
in one high-ceilinged room, I was all the fire.*

## First Sex

The way Matt Dillon and Kitty were
on *Gunsmoke*—barely touching
but giving up something offscreen
in one of those Dodge House rooms
full of light and lace, clean—
that's how I pictured it. But she
was Colombian, menstrual, barely
spoke English beyond *Bethlehem*
for *Bentley.* Matt would have
never been in that silver Airstream,
days of dishes in a stopped-up sink.
He'd have touched his Stetson, said
Ma'am and rose, faintly smelling
of leather, horses, tin marshal's
star catching the light caught her—
hair, breasts, shoulders, dark
child-nursed circles of nipple.
I woke with a burning a week later.
Matt would have had Chester limp
over to the Long Branch, fetch
a fifth and some kill-or-cure elixir,
then shot her, gentlemanly-like,
made it look like she drew down on him
first. (He'd have had to: Honor,
that other bitch of a hired gun,
would have called him out.) It's
nearly forty years, a million units
of penicillin later, but that's what I'm
doing in the street. We'll settle up
with Colts, Rosita, one of us riding off
better for living by a code binding
and more just than micro-organisms.
I'll give you that split second, sun
in your eyes, the dust of horses
settling on us dull as blood.

## The Orchard the Dry Year

*And yet if it's true, as I've read*
*that the starving body eats itself,*
*it's true it eats the heart last.*

—Katha Pollitt

In an orchard once
Bobby Ramsdail and I learned to wait.
Sisters, our mothers had moved in together:
their husbands, our fathers, gone.
His, in a Sidney jail; mine
off somewhere, remarried.

By July we'd taken to climbing
to the brown centers of trees,
wearying old oak and apple
with looking out onto the drab, flat
tabletop of Dayton, Ohio.
Any higher meant risking dry upper limbs.

George Kosta, oldest boy on the block at 13,
taught us how drought works, how
every so often it forgets to rain.
*Till someone reminds it.* Bobby and I,
drawn in, trusting,
asked instructions. *Indians stripped,*
*danced stark naked by fires. You could*
*probably get by with streetlights, maybe*
*underwear.*
               Not cruelly, I laugh now
when Bobby writes he is unhappy.
In a card I remind him of the dance—
hard, lanky bodies moving at midnight
in the middle of Comanche Drive, highest point
in Kettering—how a better vision
might have waited rain the way we did

our fathers: Bobby's, released in the fall;
mine, home in a year. Two.

Our way we had another counting
that whole month, hope,
though after each tucking in
we watched from the top bunk
the day's dry going, that hollowing,
dark to darker. The happy night
it rained, apple boughs let down
and spilled a poor failed fruit,
loose branching, the story of our lives.

Now, my cousin
who I love like a brother
phones in the night, says he'll
see me soon, that he is taking
antidepressant drugs, Lithium.
I might cry some, he says. Don't mind it.

## Bird and Miles

They have a way of talking, between bites
of fried chicken, Bird and this fine light-
skinned woman alternately eating a wing
and leaning to kiss Bird's naked thigh,
so that the taxi down to 52nd Street
fills with smacking. Bird, already high
on heroin, fans one famous hand
around the neck of a fifth, inhales
his favorite food from the loose fist
of the other. Asks Miles Davis, who's
nineteen at the most, does all this make him
just the least bit *uncomfortable.*
The woman, in light summer clothes,
a dress, heels, kneels down in daylight
until everything hums in the half heat
of the backseat. *Turn your head, Miles,*
Bird says, and Miles does. Hangs it
out the down window. Miles is wearing
the wide-lapeled suit Bird bummed last week
after pawning his own and a suitcase.
(The suit, too small, hadn't fit in the sleeves
or pants legs, and Bird had gone to the gig
at the Three Deuces looking ridiculous. Bird
played that night like he had on a tux.)
The woman fans a fly or bead of sweat
from her face. No one in the taxi
but she and Bird are moving, no one from
that other world outside where rain threatens.
Just this puffy-eyed, running-to-fat
balding black man White America has heard of
or will. This woman practicing an art
thrills all those other interiors like a breeze
sudden through a room, even in the backseat
of a taxi traveling deeper into the heart
of the delta of 1945, New York City traffic.

Finally there, everyone moves—Miles,
Bird, the woman. The driver who,
resetting the meter, watches Bird
the way you would anyone whose movements
call to mind flame, purling, blue,
jumping in the astonished air above a stove
someone's lit and turned from.

## Dizzy Gillespie at the Blue Note

*Somebody sat on his trumpet in 1953 and*
*he's been playing with a bent bell ever since.*

—*The New Yorker*

*I will take you with me. I will*
*lift you* the black balloons of his foreface
seem to say. And he does. Tosses you

like an infant, the whole exchange
having taken Time, a second child,
and tossed it toward whatever Heaven

the bent bell sends an impossible music.
Just to flower like that, once,
and go again among strangers, knowing

not only what this jazz is besides black
history blonde white women sway to
but that beauty displaces us. Bent

as if receiving other, more universally
pained sets of notes or tones,
the bell of the horn burgeons, gilt bloom

of some hope of anything like satisfaction
or even a momentary letting up of longing.
Be thankful there is no music encompassing

the one darkness makes babes of us all.
Be glad there are those so filled
to bursting that their jowl muscles weaken

and they blow it out, changed, pure.
How does this work? He owns the notes,
they cry to be loosed, he holds them forever.

## *View from the Great Southern Hotel*

Couples entwined, couples
not entirely together,

dark men and white
all manner of machine

walk and crawl unconsidered
the hard carapace, this city

where the vendors say the Bible
and American flag are always hot items.

Even if the world is finished,
snow falls on Columbus, Ohio.

Behind plastic, light-in-light-
blooming arc welders

promise superabundance
for a handful whose lives

rise piece by beautiful piece
at the decibel level of traffic.

Reinvention the rule, who
takes dominion does so by inches,

air and water
and imprecise earth overthrown,

patinaed bench attesting
quietly

to the persistence of what we put here.
What is not acceded to

becomes another freezing vision:
wide-bodied ascensions into skyline,

closing margin between field
and field. Indigenous spin a cocoon

against the spew and plenitude.
Call it adaptation. Wings of snow

on I-beams
blacken and are replaced all day.

## Letcher County, Kentucky

An hour before dawn in the coal towns in late summer
lights in the similar houses eclipse
the simple, locked-in hovering of one more day.
In the lane: rain crow, intervals of silence
and cricket singing. At this hour
the world sags. Gods and heroes, the rules
of the game bend, the more ambitious
having fenced woods and creek, private tunnels
of death-in-life. All turned or turning
to boxcars heaped black, hard extended curving lines,
an appetite for heat and night's lessening.

When coal was king, they came here dreaming.
Now, Goose Creek runs rust-red when it runs.
Killdeer seining on the wing eat nothing
in the tender fashion indigenous these days.
Underground fires near Norton, on the Virginia side,
have smoldered thirty years—a stingy, continuous burn
raveling a deeper, unmoored darkness
thread by ragged thread. All the deaths

in quiet houses—if there is Paradise, after,
we people it: Bill Barnett, going forever
after the same one loaf of bread
leading from Elkhorn Coal to four years in the Navy,
sons Doug and Billy at light's edge
in the same dark, forgiving God, forgiven,
no heaven apart from these lesser evidences of grace.

Yet in some cerebral folding or chemical recess
we know—in the way rock holds, in the way it's all
work—if hope were coal seams we'd mine willingly.
As it is, we buy big-kneed Joyce Yontz a print dress,
take it to her, drunk already.
If she's laughing, drunk herself, all the better.

## The Picture My Father Promised

A true story. Ever since my father
brought home the black oak framed
faces of Quiller and Ellen Bentley,
my sadly human, homely even, great-
grandparents, I listened with interest

to the half-truths of our family history.
The picture had been tinted
in a way that made Quiller and Ellen
appear made-up, nineteenth century.
I can't tell from the photograph

what either of them thought of this life,
but my father becomes noticeably sad
then strangely buoyant when he speaks
of the picture or his boyhood. As if
the fact his mother went berserk

and had to be institutionalized
soon after his birth, says nothing
of the love in these two faces.
These are the two who locked his mother
in an upstairs room on learning

of her pregnancy by a married man.
Who first shuttled her off
to the sanitarium in Lexington
when all she really was was angry.
My father knows this. Knows I know.

He knew the afternoon he promised the picture
and all the ambiguity attending it.
We used to have to take his mother
back to Kentucky and the sanitarium.
She used to sit in the backseat

of our '48 Mercury—aloof, a shadow
passing across her face before the anger
broke in waves and she called me
"little son-of-a-bitch" out of the blue.
It was always nightfall

when we left her, always evening
and hard to read my father's face
on the drive home to Ohio. The light
from the dashboard subtracted everything
except his eyes, and even they glowed

with a light not of this world or the next
but some distant huddling together at last,
all our deaths and lives turned to one life
we fall through, the only warmth
handed over in a dark car.

# III

*from* **The Trouble With**
**a Short Horse in Montana**

## The Whore Is Born in Texas

It starts with the butts we're field-stripping
in a rolling motion between thumb and index finger,
tobacco and filter floss scattered
in no special direction onto flat squadron lawns.
Someone's told us to police the area.

The first black guy I've spoken to in my life
wants to talk, says he's from Detroit.
The next step is mine: *I've taken LSD
at least twenty times, but I can't get laid.*
There's no premeditation to it, no scheming;

this is everything true I know to say.
He says, You're a damn holy man.
He's got a big gap-toothed smile, looks
like a short Malcolm X in Air Force fatigues.
(I've read about Malcolm in *Life* magazine.)

It starts to rain, big drops, and he tells me
if we ever get leave he'll show me
a place in town, all the tricks. We're
getting soaked, more so by the minute.
He says his name's Leonard, but

that I should call him Butch. Says
he'll call me Whore in the same way
they call big men Tiny. I like him.
*You smoke?* I ask. There's that no-apologies
smile you can buy whatever you need with.

I don't think: Gee, we're going to be friends.
I think this broad, flat nose a very perfect bird's
wing, his expression that of a kid playing hooky.
Not cigarettes, he says, letting go leaf
into that other life of west Texas wind.

## News of God

Pre-dawn, late February. Lines of uniforms and
the voices of boots, base streets a second flesh
of ice. There's little to do this early
but half-step and pray. He's short, Butch,
in the rear of the column, says later that he

sees me falling to earth, disappearing abruptly
up ahead in the blue dark. This night
is ice for miles running, and it's forcing
big men and small to call *Christ Jesus*
and reach for whomever's at hand. Or nothing.

I can see the glare as off of a lake
whose still surface receives the weight of men.
It's like a movie, guys in snaking lines
making a hole for the fallen. Say you've
fallen, sit amazed, and no one will stop. No one.

Suddenly, the dark behind those on the road
opens to extend a merciful hand and *Wham*—
you both go down. Say you're both laughing now,
or else you're about to, and this hand's
still holding on. You want it to release

but you need it. The thing is you can't, finally,
go on without help. Something else: you fall,
rise, fall, and keep giving orders to God
or Heaven concerning the disposition
of all this ice, the indifferent season,

a shiny-with-starlight state of Texas
that has turned a kind of silver underfoot.
In that moment the air itself parts, yields.
It knows about keeping its balance, about
distances traveled in a whole other country.

## The Politics of Spit

Without our uniforms, the haircuts
betray everything: we're *servicemen*
and enlistees since no one gets drafted
into the Air Force, which makes us doubly
hated in Champaign, Illinois in 1973.
It's the Ray-Bans and white-sidewall, trimmed-
around the ears hair-length in the Age
of Aquarius. Still, I'm stunned when someone
lets go a huge you-know that lands at our
feet then a smaller one that hits me
like the realization America isn't one country.
We're just standing there, stupefied, checking
ourselves like the ones in the Real War
must have had to after a fire fight. A command
to oneself not to fold, not here, little coins
of cruelty abloom on this broadcloth shirt.
It is when I stand like this—
shamed, changed forever, past the splatter,
that I feel what it is to be taken in
by an idea of one's own worthiness,
to die to that and learn about the nature
of Power and its companion Humiliation.
I think this stuff soaks in, and it does.
Marked this way, I can begin.

## The Gratitude of Snakes

You had to feed the thing a rat.
And often it wouldn't get anywhere near
*That* rat, for reasons known
Only to snakes. Instead,

While the rat huddled, watching,
The snake struck thick aquarium glass
Or your exposed hand—

To remind you what was wild in that room.

You got bit, careful or not, and it stung.
Ask Ralph Hupp: I wouldn't call what happened
To his face a kiss of thanks. Nothing

Like the old antagonisms rising in an air
Of pure surprise. Nothing like
A man tugging at the snake on his face,
The snake on his face holding on

As if they were, together, snake and man,
One mouth trying to swallow. You know
A big, pained *God Almighty* went out.

And from the two sets of eyes—
Seeing as for the first time—
That same light that always escapes.

## Unfit

Where I went, after they were through
taking back the uniforms, breaking my heart,
was to Ohio, my parents' home,
with the crisp October air to soften
all that disgrace, the overarching sycamores
of the better-of-two roads into town
dusting me with leaf-scent and sun and a lack of gloom

and dropping palm-sized tokens onto the shoulders
of pedestrians, hero and outlier alike, raining
down a golden message: you can outlast anything.
My father said: *You've shamed us.* Everyone else
was weary of talk of war and the calamity
of Southeast Asia. There was sufficient shame
to go around; the pallbearers of another America

buried the best of themselves, went back to work
walking stiffly toward ruined futures. Loss builds,
by definition, as monument every day. I took
a job bending pipe until the blood raced again.
The ache of being futureless was freeing; I worked
16-hour shifts, all the overtime they'd give me,
until they laid the whole lot of us off that Christmas.

They said: We've got enough pipe for now. Happy
Holidays. And snow fell in wet-heavy handfuls
through sycamores wanting nothing, wishless,
or wanting only to be what they were, unbowed.
There's just so much bending you can do, it turns out.
As if anyone could be found fit for his life, could bend
to fit this life; fill it like a suit of clothes, or uniform.

## Why Palestinian Men Fire Submachine Guns in the Direction of the Bone-Colored Face of the Man in the Moon

They have forgotten physics and the Qur'an
of gravity. Bullets go up like prayers: a sky and
faint stars concede only that there are rules to this.
It's nightfall; barrel flashes light the storefronts
and stone streets of Bethlehem. Sometimes
peace is an absolution of little thunders by a shop
that can't keep posters of Clint Eastwood in stock.
Sometimes the sun sets like the end of a Western.

Even now, a soccer star's fugitive brother
sleeps in a different neighbor's house each night
to avoid arrest, re-imprisonment. Sometimes
he dreams of his 46-year-old mother in a hospital,
dying alone, compassion the property of those
who can call down God as border guards. Tonight,
a radio of explosives on a shoulder hails a taxi.
*Oh, turn it up,* someone says. *American music.*

## The Wreck of the Barbie Ferrari

—*John Hiatt*

Ken is standing in the mall parking lot
next to a carload of Mexicans when I get in
and take his place beside Barbie Millicent Roberts.
She wears something nautical, blue-white, designer,
those rocket breasts heartbreaking in profile.
We listen to jazz as she puts the machine
through its paces. She has a way with it,
but it is her nonchalance in traffic
says she is talented, blessed with good reflexes
and a tartarless smile. I put my tongue
in her perfect mouth at a four-way stop.
She says not to do that; I do it again.
It feels like I need to do *something* and,
besides, Ken did wave his model's wave
of acceptance resting on endless opportunity.
Either it's my imagination or she kisses back,
but we're kissing when she swerves
at 130 or more on a two-lane, pretending
she can drive and make love and downshift.
The girl has no idea of death, but she knows
some tricks as if avoidance of disaster
were a major and her Ivy League education
in becoming invisible a sort of secret shared.
We're clear. But then she parts her legs-by-Mattel
and her summer shorts ride up and she reaches
between the seat and her anatomical promise of
a WMD. I barely feel the impact, and I can tell you
that leaving this world is incremental, wishful thinking,
though it begins in terror and glancing upward.
When was the afternoon anything but a dull ache?
When did it begin to rain and you not notice
the blood river beside you smelled of setting gel?
She could use some help. We both could.

## The Trouble with a Short Horse in Montana

### 1

Your father is sitting with friends
at 3 a.m. in a Howard Johnson's,
watching a wall of white brick accept the cold.
Someone else from the closing air base
says, Who said the Cold War is over?
There are doughnuts and a German chocolate cake
pedestaled on a counter of Formica and chrome
and a glass pot of coffee on a warmer.
A cook slides a plate of eggs and toast
through the smoke of endless low-tar cigarettes.
A waitress figures tax and pretends
not to listen to arguments for and against
Joe Montana being God Almighty. Outside,
the four lanes of the state route steam
with a salting of snow going up whole.
The brute voices of truck engines sound, busted-hearted,
the pump lights out at a Clark station, the still block
the small brilliances of business signs. The eyes
of the waitress fill with one November night.
She could smile at your father, but it wouldn't help.

2

It's his weekend and I'm free to roam
the lot and lift-bays of his service station.
There is a woman in a wedding dress at the pumps
and the white numbers click incrementally.
The fueling hose is back on the hook:
something from the dripping nozzle goes up
like any heady kitchen scent—bread
or gingerbread or pinto beans simmering all day.
There are pyramids of cans that point to a great need
broad and thick as bearing grease or oil leavings
on the floor of the bay where they come
to be made new or good as new.
There's a stock room where hydraulic hissings
compress the hour, impossibly, into a hand—
I sleep through the late-night raisings and lowerings
that begin each overhaul under the hum of electric light.
Finally, I sleep through the song of the pump bell.
They say the Hubble telescope has recorded Creation's holy shine
riding the bang of the first gaseous instants. I'm waiting
for the thread-scripted *Roy* on the pocket of a uniform.

3

I had come prepared to watch Gene Autry
vault onto Champion and ride through fire.
Gene could have strummed "Tumbling Tumbleweeds"
and I know I would have forgiven him anything.
He arrived late. It rained. I see a bunch of kids
ushered from the grandstand into lines
to a tent where the air stank instantly
of horse shit. This wasn't my dream of America.
One kid, getting soaked, said, *This ain't Trigger.*
I didn't say anything. The rain had doused
the infield; rain ran into my cowboy boots.
But, inside the tent, Gene Autry got up
on the back of his famous horse. Said
we could, too. And I took a turn, six years old
and frightened to death of horses.
There were cowboys and cowgirls, a tentful
from all over Montgomery County, Ohio. Unmoored,
tent sides flapped and rose like the skirt of that other movie star.
Whatever else I have, Gene Autry is all smiles.
There was, or there wasn't, another ride.

## 4

When you consider the scrap biscuits, the act itself
of apportioning what's at hand and the flouring pat
and reforming of what might have been one thing, loaves,
but will do nicely, thank you, as this other—
when you consider that an ancient wrist at forehead
brushing back the errant strand of hair pauses
and that nothing else is lost in pausing; when you
consider the absolute abundance of inner resource
in the face of one so accustomed to sighing, that a face
is as much light as anything; when you consider
the thousand failures of heart absorbed by the blood,
that such a multitude of disappointments becomes a self
and fuels the unillumined in us in the way a stubborn fire catches;
when you consider the O of the mouth shaping its own
new sound and phoneme for *You can't win,* that noise
of that sort is exactly what mercy should fly to
like a mother to a newborn's loud testimony to want;
when you consider how absence wracks a body
regardless of size or shape or age, that it is to suckle
we want and not be turned away, then

5

we hear the cry of the believer-fallen-from-belief
as beginning and not the final word on God
or our lives in the light and the other work of hearts,
which is the bread we expect like the next sun, the next,
and we are permitted only so much joy for the reason
that we would stand and feast and crowd the table,
though the rest starved and went to bed hungry, wincing
at the inequalities God is maker of, and because saying
and singing for our place at the feast would pass away,
lift and fall, like the breasts of this one so broken
and yet breaking off her grief in the way weather changes.
Suddenly I am listening to what it means to be here.
All night there has been talk of demons and sin
and Myrtle, my aunt Myrtle, has prayed and sang
but now this morning she is up making biscuits.
Flour rises in bright divinations on the wind of her motion,
of her working out her rage at the death of my uncle,
even that become something extra for a child up early
who watches as if hungry for something besides bread, though
bread should be religion enough, Eucharist and resurrection.

# 6

Because all one summer I prayed to fly—
first in the orchard, and always on a branch
when I loved the dirt as much as any kid
apprenticed to aloneness, a journeyman at 9
graduated to talking aloud to himself or singing
those songs of love the transistor resonated with.
Just an idea, as they say. Then I began to ask
and imagine an itching as with new skin—
now and again the random leaping of faith, groundward,
from high enough up I could have been killed
but wasn't, which led to more praying and falling
because I believed I kept company with God Himself.
I blame the orchard. It was too beautiful, too
quiet—a kind of house of monastic bliss boys crave
like the neighbor girl's breasts. I filled it with prayer
of a lion-hearted sort, as in *Hey, you, Old Man.*
It hardly matters now. It so happens
I got my fill of bruised fruit and getting
bruised myself; it was expensive, believing,
but I fooled that place in the brain flashes DANGER

7

another, clearer voice telling me to forget it, forget
all about wings. After so long, you see your impression
in the grasses and get the idea. I got it.
I saw that I was alone in the orchard.
I saw that the only wings I was sprouting
were the raised places where rock had found flesh
and flesh had grown angelic, all right—wings of dislocations,
pairs of bruises blue as summer sky, yellow sprains,
black-yellow like a June apple gone at the core.
And sore—I couldn't walk without suffering again
each failure, each unanswered asking. I felt
God's great deafness with every step. I *believed*—
but you learn. I knew the real and present pain
of there being nothing and no one to catch you. I knew
the only hand that would break my fall banged limbs
unmercifully all the way down. Then
I was still moving, still alive; I had flown
all we ever fly on faith. I saw the weight
of the body was mine to cart around a while.
I wear the rock-scars, I can tell you.

## 8

A taxi, Chevy engine as voice, that voice
of dead metals shushed in the 6 a.m. fog,
from either white door of the taxi the hand-
lacquered word GLORY leaping out at you,
blue-black, blooming in the ordinary morning air.
If you were thirty-nine, say forty,
and had escaped a failing marriage for a few days
of friendship with a woman, you might
wake early, unwilling to sleep soundly
in the wide bed of a not-so-bad hotel room.
You might rise, as I did, dress quietly,
and go about in the fine chill of early March
to think life all right again or pretty good.
You might watch street traffic, patient as stone,
so that when the light called to you, like this,
with a single word signifying victory
or recognition after long trial, some sure sign,
you were there to receive it. Nothing more.
There is a world, after all, wants what you want.
The triumph, a fierce heart. Nothing less.

## 9

I think of my pregnant, just-deserted mother
smoking a cigarette, sitting on a sofa
dissolved now into memory, the power off
and the house dark, all the clocks hushed and
showing the hour and minute after which
nothing moved ever again because someone
loved us. We can't write ourselves
out of our unhappier times. I'm there,
a presence; I do not have to imagine it.
So much of loss is what lives with us
after what lived with us is gone. I'll see,
always, her rising to walk the cold linoleum,
the lights in the other houses coming on
in the living room's black tiles. I do not
ask for mercy for myself in this life—
only the heart the body uses to cross
and recross this dark room, love's
floorshows and tricks having broken the bank,
the light bearing witness, a weight like smoke
having fallen away or been sidestepped.

## 10

According to the majority of astronomers,
a constant breeze of dark matter
blows through us, the forever-dust of Creation,
the something we know nothing of, a glue-like
gravity of spiraling little-boy-lost bodies
tugged to and fro like the star themselves.
A boy said once, in his sleep beside me,
with regard to the absolute tirelessness
of evil and death flying around out here—
I filled in the subject—*It stalks you.*
I know: it sounds too old for a child,
but he said it. And the total amount of light
in the room where he slept, sleeps yet,
they say speaks through a sulphurous haze
of secrets gravitating outward, ring-like,
a faint thunder rolling or the echoing
15-billion-year-old rumble of God
stomping the Universe into shape.
Something dreamed of whispered beside you.
Something a boy says to no one in the night.

11

They always look for it. Always.
They start from wanting to know
which road, which turn, how far, where,
to praying to any obvious marker to show them.
They have been hunting landmarks forever,
since that first looking up. This marker
is a poem against absolute closure, against lostness
and limit and death, against darkness
and getting and staying lost
while there is gas yet in the tank, fire
in the good engine that beats like a better heart.
The whole pentagonal starfish of its light
is a poem of arrivings and homecomings,
of places to come just up the road.
That light falls on the free-flow of travelers.
I was in Nebraska, stopped by a rail line,
car after rocking car challenging the singings of geese,
one light on in the Badlands Motel,
when it came to me: there is forgiveness
in going. And if no forgiveness, going.

## 12

Here between the sound of scythes
and noon-faced singing, another poor one
aches from bending while imagining
he were in a better, fairer country.
There is nothing fair or unfair about how light,
sinking along the honor prison of this row
and the next, inches past as if lost.
There is no loneliness in the single-mindedness
of leaves or a far-off dog barking,
but if he stops trying to shape the heart of him
he will cry. He may well laugh and listen
to the deep drumming sound of bass notes
unreeling above the common grasses. But release
of breath isn't joy, and there's work to be done.
No, he may as well not dream or one of those
shaking shadows infinitely expanding will claim him
and all the regret he harvests here like wheat.
It isn't that a star above a road is monument
to nothing and no one, all he gets.
It isn't that we die, then it is.

## 13

Either it's too much or truly magical, her turning
herself, but cartwheels have never looked like
something off the Playboy Channel, and she knows
she has your undivided attention. To call this
fantastic in the face of an eclipse's hesitating blush
would be to miss her eyes, older than motion,
and no one you know, loved or not,
ever laughed at the whole universe by doing what
makes perfect sense. Today, the unusual
is on schedule in the fortunate heavens overhead,
and the light looks like you're wearing Ray-Bans.
When she next extends, her closed fist of a sex
opens and the May-lit room holds its breath.
That pinkness deeper in bright as any sun, the push
and roll toward better days what the heart asks for.
If release of joy were light, you'd be bathed in it.
If love were this simple rotation, you'd turn and turn.
They say there is something rare in this presentation.
I say they should have someone so committed to delight.
It is just the two of you, and one hates getting dressed.

## 14

A postcard of a cowboy neck-deep in snow:
*The Trouble with a Short Horse in Montana*—
I can hear a son's belly laugh above other voices.
We have been five days on the road, driving,
but he is glad again, and part of the world.
Someone has pumped a dollar's worth on the ground,
someone whose weariness announces
that something in us was not born to travel.
Talking with a woman on the pay phone in back
I let the field of flowers in a voice
become a name for where we are headed.
Perhaps the cowboy on the card is happy;
I suppose he is delighted to be outdoors
where all that whiteness is country he can travel through.
That scene is funny for the time it takes
to pay for a fill-up and Mountain Dews.
The boy leading the way is tired. Getting in,
on his side, I fix one of the cards
so he can glance up and smile, if he cares to,
the next however many miles.

## What Keats' Motives Were in Studying Medicine Are Not Known with Any Certainty

—Joseph Epstein, "*The Medical Keats*"

In the garden of the hospital
someone has paced a level, flat place
in grasses to the right of an entrance
resolving whether to take this or a less-
tracked course through the world. A row
of evergreen flash in light they belong to.
Keats attends to a cigar, firing the end
and describing a circle with a long lit match.
Torrents of smoke rage and disperse.

If ecstatic loss shivers the hand
trims a temporal artery, what then?
Shall the just-dead invite tentative
and exploratory flights into *materia medica*?
He may be recalling a cauterization:
banks of smoke spreading quick shadows
and a dark at the core. Poetry—
not the stench of wounds but the story

of all wounding—may have risen above a body
and into the bad air. Failing to know
everything might have called into question
where the lancet goes, and doesn't. Moreover,
there would have been the unfiltered agony
glazing a pair of eyes, the residue of death.
Beauty and death, is it even a contest? It is
the first anniversary of the day he penned

a sonnet, the poem as lifeless as market fish,
and he may be thinking of that short visit
to a house he seemed to belong in. As if

the better prescription for pain's cessation
were a deep swallowing, and words. He seems
to have a knack for staying with a thing, igniting
again the end of his cigar. Sighing at the truth
of a glow in a garden at noon only the beginning.

## The Heron Tattoo

When I think of summer in Seattle, I think
of the tattoo parlor on Evergreen Way
in Everett, Washington, where Gloria Regalbuto
paid eighty dollars to have a Great Blue Heron
tattooed above her right breast, in four colors,
in answer to the tiger above my left breast.
I had never watched anyone being tattooed—
you can't really watch when they do it to you—
and I saw blood rise up from her, oxygenated,
bright, sulphur-colored, the never-completed blood
of her history and her apprenticeship to it.
She bled her mother's cruelty, the lesser bumps
of girlhood in Cleveland's Little Italy; she bled
her artist-father's successes, his failures, the art
of being able to talk Cleveland Browns football
from a hospital bed; she bled the surface of her face
changing from stunningly beautiful to just beautiful
to the uncertain nights lessening its best features;
she bled early menses, Catholic school, the lie
that pain is your ticket to Heaven. Then, it slowed;
the work was done—the rainbow-outline of body
restricted to shades of blue and deep-forest green,
the white top-beard of the bird's head, the legs
so identifiable as Bird as to be nearly a caricature.
When I think of love, being loved,
that's what I see, that bruise of a bird
standing on a lakeshore of flesh and seeing
itself and the world in eyes that happen to be
looking down, trying to disappear into another
whose blood's mirror is theirs and shining
with what is and isn't about to fly.

## Motorcade

Four-positioned American flags, 48-starred,
flap in the air before and behind my father's
'56 Cadillac DeVille, snap from the big chrome lip
of a front grille. The road ahead
is a line of like-minded Korean War veterans
motorcading to Frankfort to tell Bert Combs,
50th governor, that just because the only work
is in Ohio, nothing changes the fact
the State of Kentucky owes its veterans *something*.

We have the PA system. A bank of tubes blooms
to life on the floor between the seats—a voice,
my father's, booms out how we're almost there.
Nettie, my mother, brushes my short hair. Says
we'll be stopping for cheeseburgers and Co-colas.
We're following this red Merc with black tailfins
I bet would be boring to God after a while.
My father won't tell us, for years yet, what he's seen
in the service of this his country. If there are words,
then they're barked out directions, orders

to the other cars, his big voice otherworldly and
traveling now alongside the motorcade,
in the passing lane of this brand-new interstate.
Glassed in this way, for all I know at 5, we're
on our way to Alabama and a civil rights march.
But there are no black faces in the cars
that have crossed again into Kentucky, their homeland,
to get what's theirs. There was the guy with hooks
for hands who could drive a car, his luminous face
nothing to do with loss. And the soon-to-be-judge lawyer
from Dayton who might as well have been Abraham Lincoln.
And, of course, they got their money. Every cent.
I got this memory of my father that will not die.
He's the voice shouts to the world, You owe me money!

when all Bert Combs needed was the redneck equivalent
of Martin Luther King, Jr. calling him "a son-of-a-bitch
politician" at noon on the capitol steps. Whoever
he saw my father to be, standing on the hood of a Cadillac,
breezes blowing his Kentucky Colonel necktie to one side
in the middle of the tangle of cars below, he went
down. To shake hands and promise him anything.

*from* **Starlight Taxi**

## Elegy, Neon Junction

On the Google map, there's a cement-block building—
last I heard, in '06, it was a Double Kwik Market—
and, beside it, a scar of a road to a mountainside
of laurel and live oak and a grid of tombstones.
If it's still there, the black gate swings in-only.
A majority of the markers bear the name Bentley.
*Friends & loved ones, we are gathered here today*
may not echo above the hollows of Letcher County,
above double-wide trailers and desolate row houses
with their warning that this life is a train of sorrow
and that steep cliffs and poor footing make the rules,

but the newest slab of granite reads *Beloved mother*
because my sentimental father didn't want this one
reduced to an urn of ashes and scattered in Florida.
For him, death and the sleep of the dead aren't wed
to mystery as much as to a hillside acre overlooking
Neon Junction and Doc Bentley Road, the Double
Kwik Market off Highway 317 and Highway 805.
The place is there for those who know where to look
and why that shiver up the spine isn't about wind
or reminders that we die but what it takes to live
where all the talk is an inventory of close escapes.

## Men Coming Out of a Mine

The foreman takes a shuttle car out, rides
as far as the squat orange thing is going.
The rest are walking, in no great hurry,
into the quiet and magnitude of late day.
That one hates all dogs because he sees
himself as treated with far less respect.
Laughing, he lists into another walker.
That one in a Ben Roethlisberger jersey
kicks a Mountain Dew bottle that sprays
a face that runs mask-black below a tipple
and conveyor in the Elkhorn coal fields.
Dashiell Hammett describes a prizefighting
arena in a mining town called Poisonville—
*Smoke. Stink. Heat. Noise.* Like that. Maybe
not so much smoke at the moment but add
'mean' since that's what coal mining does
to some men: makes them mean. If asked,
they'd call what all this is—*fun.* Booyah.
Fifteen minutes of grab-ass at shift change.
They know what they look like, swinging
dinner buckets with Obama-Biden stickers,
tossing around the latest Rush Limbaugh lie
or news of the hanging of a census worker.
That limping one sidesteps idling machinery,
the apparatus contributing to some scrubbing
of the methane from the air in the mountain.
The lastlight of day has maybe an hour to go,
so they hurry to be rid of the mines. To save
a little of themselves for a night of *Shake that!*
If I didn't have to stop, their movements say,
but all of them get in line at the time clock by
the lockers. Even shadows want to leave here.

## Incident Involving a Hoe Handle

There they are, standing in a garden near Goose Creek,
there's Billy, both his turreted Potter ears protruding
in the slant sun of a June evening in eastern Kentucky,
turning under fresh manure in his washed-out overalls,
abundant rain and a month's neglect having made a surf
of native grasses (and fly-buzz) through which he steps,
a boy with memories of having run away with the circus
until a roustabout escorted him onto an eastbound train,

and there's Nettie with that younger-sister snarl of hers,
Jean Harlow—taller—with mustard-gold hair. She weeds
a row of half-runner beans half-heartedly, complaining.
There's heat, though it isn't the purgatorial Southern sort.
She hisses at him. She wants to practice her jump shot.
Lives for the small-town crowd roar at the minor miracle
of a 12-footer landing. She says, *I quit.* Tosses the hoe.
In an aerial view of Fleming-Neon, the town, her refusal

would be important only in the way that what happens
to an ant is hugely important to the future of that one ant.
Her brother wipes sweat. And bends to pick up the hoe
that begs him to settle the score—and swings. Nettie
goes down like she's been tackled; a scream she lets fly
says there are truths and that pain is chief among them.
Knowing there will be hell to pay, he takes off running.
Glances back as though expecting his wronged sister

to be waving a busted hoe handle. All these years later,
I call them home from that garden to replay the whipping
my uncle says he got for raising train-track red welts
on the backs of my mother's calves. To see for myself
what the solemn and ecclesiastical sun found in them,
my high-spirited mother and uncle. Which was a heart
equal to its share of the undeserved beatings in a life,
this circus of miracles you can't quit or walk away from.

*Faced with Starvation, Who Wouldn't Want to Say,*
*Check the Oil and Fill 'er Up?*

Kentuckians, my people, may not have known the road
but they had jalopies. They didn't care what factory
they landed in. They trailered a perfectly swaying dream
of fair-wage futures, houses with postage-stamp yards
where they might garden. They got the job; and, after work,
filled dark, dangerous bars with names like The Well. It wasn't
enough they worked double shifts, all the offered overtime;

they were punished with names like *briar hopper* and *hillbilly*,
pride a fat wallet and an Eldorado or Coupe DeVille
with white-sidewalled Firestone tires. They courted their kind
in Northern dancehalls; they laughed too loud at a *reckon*
or *yonder* or *y'all* from voices that owned them
irrespective of breast size or looks. No trick of the night
canceled the depth of such connectedness. They talked

fatback and beans. And caught a whiff of coal smoke
and were persuaded that Happiness wasn't a full belly
but a state of mind situated south of the Ohio River.
They'd made it out of the Hills but only to be MIA
in an unrecognizable America. They were prisoners,
as were their offspring, for generations. A homeland
wasn't what they fought for but moments of belonging

and secular blessing in which bankers didn't question
a man's ability to save so much of nothing. They might
clear land of trees that toppled like towers. So what
if they died heartbroken, too young even to finish
paying for the Cadillac in the drive. There's luck
and a dream of cool water when you're thirsty.
And there's getting to work to dig the well.

## Being from Dayton

We are in flight here. We've come looking for runways.
Pastures flatten under us, wildflowers beaten down
by contraptions dropped from the barely navigable air.
Indigenous are offspring of the Freedom Railroad,
Ohio the yes vote for a future where wide-eyed looks
count for nothing or are overtaken by what's real
and jobs that grow on trees beside the still waters.

Dayton used to be home to the Wright Brothers.
The Belmont Drive-In Theatre, stories of light
and the unforeseen. Roy's Shell on Wilmington.
Fear of loss made families of strangers
then silent strangers of the same families
made to witness the end of a dream of something
ripped up like yard weeds by factory work.

The whole of my heart is Appalachian
and means never to settle anywhere. I keep a
pair of suitcases packed, being from Dayton. My
youngest sister manages a mall. My other sister
makes loans for Bank One. They're pissed-off
at the world, like my mother, from loving
this place (and the last) and having to uproot.

One by one we pack up and leave the city,
the suburbs, Kettering and Trotwood, all the houses
it took our best efforts to buy, some beautiful,
some so undeniably ugly as to be eyesores,
stains upon an already-trampled landscape. We think
surely Wright-Patt, the air base, will save us
with a civil service job and retirement in Fairborn,
this city of servants; of slaves, really.
We are from Dayton. We don't like to fly.
We know Wilbur Wright died in a landed bed,
of influenza, a sickness born of close contact

with other humans, then crowd in together to work
in aerospace museums, at Daimler-Chrysler. Being away
from Dayton we see we are visiting air shows, the dead
in their sky-blue uniforms. We're embarrassed at having
fallen into place in yet another long, slow-moving line
of outerbelt traffic past new-development bare fields.

## King of Ghosts

I'm said to be descended from the Plantagenets. Edward II.
Twenty-five generations or so back. My grandmother Potter.
Mazy Frances Collier Potter wove her ashen hair into a bun
for the Old Regular Baptist services in McRoberts, Kentucky.
I was never in attendance for what she said took place there.
Outdoors, in summer, under skies buttressed by laurel thickets
in uncanvassed sunlight for which there aren't words. A place
out of the backwoods of James Dickey's novel *Deliverance*.
Some of our people had houses with earthen floors I walked
and walk now, in memory, smelling soup beans simmering.

She had no idea we had been sired by Edward Plantagenet
who, at the time, was wed to Isabella de France. She would
have been keeping an eye on her cornbread on the black stove
and one eye on the chubby boy she took with her in those days.
Kings would have had no use for her or ham-hocked soup beans
and cornbread. Or her religion, which was all about the mountains,
though it claimed to be about heaven. The avoidance of damnation.
I'd take a bowl of soup beans and a wedge of anything warm from
her hands over a throne. And fuck the blood proving nothing except
that I exist, progeny of those who recognized loss like the sounds

of some untranslatable heavenly tongue. I was her shadow then.
But how could I know she'd leave me in a world about to have
happen to it what happens to the character in that Dickey novel,
the Bobby character, a salesman, who is raped in his pale ass
by the mountain man who thinks it's his right because he can.
I don't want to think of that just now, the fate of this world
or the truly awful things that befall any of us. I want to recall
what she offered me from the door in a Glenwood coal stove
kindled by wood shavings or pages of *The Mountain Eagle*
balled up, put to good use. Something memorable and fine.

## Mirror, Brush & Comb

In a rectangle of window light that falls on her bed
my grandmother Bentley sits unwrapping gifts.

This is a day of ribbons and patterned paper
dropped like currency at the feet of a woman.
The next opened box holds the gilded tools
of looking presentable. She hands it back,
saying, *Oh, honey, this is too nice for me.*
I'm a kid; I know to say nothing and watch.

My mother takes the box, stepping into the sun's
idea of the true and beautiful in Ohio in December.
Whatever light doesn't fall on her divvies itself
into a fractious Braille on the chenille bedspread.
I watch my mother place the present on the bed.
And I see it takes patience to live in this world.

How long will this gift-giving go on? Longer
than a boy of five accepts without fidgeting.

Still, you ought to have seen what I saw—
a woman rumored to have shot at a man,
working her tongue against a last remaining tooth:
a figure spent from storybook disappointments:
a stranger with white hair and a look on her face
I can only describe as fierce, reaching at last

for what's been mislaid. As if it were love,
precious in the stiff fingers of either hand.

## Hell for Certain, Kentucky

> *Oh, do not ask, "What is it?"*
> *Let us go and make our visit.*
>
> —T.S. Eliot, "The Love Song of J. Alfred Prufrock"

On your way to collect a pension check
in Neon or from that other p.o. box in Whitesburg
your meager need sends you to, the need not to be beholding
to another human being, you detour for a cold drink.
As a girl, years ago, you heard the crows in Hell for Certain
sing "Amazing Grace," or so you say, loopy from a night
without sleep on a Greyhound bus. And here you are,
fifty or so miles off the beaten track, sweating in the July sun
before air-conditioning, swiveling around on a fountain bar stool
to catch the attention of a waitress popping her Beeman's gum
as she steps around you, order pad in hand, on her way elsewhere.
Her hair isn't gray-white, like yours, though it's pinned back
and twisted in a tight bun as black as your Samsonite suitcase.

*Honey*, you say, *two Co-colas.* Because I'm there too, beside you,
five, six, and you don't mean to let anyone be so rude
thinking either you're old or not from around here.
But it's no good. She's locked on to the cabbie brought you,
who holds his Pall Mall like an over-the-hill James Dean:
like the next drag of his cigarette will send him somewhere exotic
and maybe she could go, too. Anywhere but Whitesburg.

You smile again, and her white-uniformed presence spins,
looks you dead in the eyes as if to ask *Bitch, what the hell is it?*
while the Seeburg hi-fi speakers at the counter spew
an Everly Brothers tune. Outside a wall-of-window plate glass
a coal truck grinds its gears, coughing to a stop at the pumps
as if a good case of black lung commenced with inbreathing
all that kicked-up dust from the unpaved state route—

there's always a spark of recognition in a memory like this,
and you'd curse at the busty waitress if it would do any good
or I wasn't on the next bar stool, clutching a Teddy bear
I'll mislay later on the steps of the Letcher County Courthouse.

## Funerals in the South

We didn't sing "My Old Kentucky Home" or "Dixie,"
but we might as well have. Without fail, neighbors
poured in with Tupperware-sealed Texas sheet cakes,
Jell-O, to-die-for fried chicken, ham, pecan pie. Grief,
it turns out, swallows easier than you might think.
I can tell you now the adults scared us, the children,
opening their hearts to loss. The scariest of mourners
had to be Myrtle, my aunt, a holy-roller fond of saying
Satan had her by the throat—she called him *Beelzebub*,
as though a sort of respect or friendship had sprung up.
At the eulogy—hellfire and damnation were preached
over our dead who, by *God*, had to listen—she'd raise
a bony arm to signify that the Holy Ghost, "the Spirit,"
was upon her. Sooner or later, shouting *Je-sus! Je-sus!*
until it echoed in the funeral home like a braking train
whose wheel-song of descent calls to mind journeys,

an end to journeying. If the casket was closed, she'd
pound a lid; if it was open, she'd take hold of a hand
or trace the rouged-and-powdered contours of a face.
Thankfully, she had limits. Mouths were sacrosanct.
No smooching the chill lips of the Departed. Which
I understood, even then: a body's temperature after
embalming isn't a thing to have register at any age.
If April is the cruelest month, then it's always April
in some part of eastern Kentucky. I wanted to sing:
*Weep no more my lady. Oh! Weep no more today!*
But I was a kid. I sang what and when I was told.
If there's a God, enthroned in some obscene palace,
weeping because one Cross and Savior isn't enough,
not in the coal towns, then she was right to sign on
as cheerleader. If not, there's the solace of food—
napkins under chins to catch the hallelujah crumbs.

# Grief, Joy Mingle at Snake Handler's Funeral

*A whisper allows us to hear the most sound.*

—David Baker

Wind is once again ghosting around outside,
and as lovers rub and nuzzle by a coffee-maker
in Viewing Room Two, by the closed casket,
I begin to think about the taking up of serpents
spoken of in the Book of Mark, where I first
learned that the history of the Western World
is an all-or-nothing, here-and-gone history.

According to the eulogy, Reverend Jessop
was a furloughed miner used to making do:
like his Lord and Savior who had to reattach
an ear in dark Gethsemane to prove we are
out of place in our ill-fitting miracle skin.
Donnie Jessop's blue suit is a poor fit, too,
after years grieving the loss of his job and

that tall brunette by the cups and creamer.
If all breath is the shared breath of God,
Reverend J. might have done well to let go
and not look heavenward and wait to register
what had happened, how the rattler whisper-
hissed as venomous rattlers will, striking
because it was pissed and because it could.

Trusting the promise that the first to die
are the first resurrected, it never occurred
to Donnie that the Lord might look away
as he draped the thing around his bare neck
and a fine fury of teeth became a theology
of the work of the body. Which began
where the work of the spirit left off.

*Life Lessons (Dayton, Ohio, 1963 - 1966)*

After the Cuban Missile Crisis and JFK's assassination
my parents called it quits. I lived with my mother
in the house he left her to hold onto as best she could,
which she filled with her anger. Even at 9 years old
I knew how hard it is just to live and breathe.
My mother was a master of recovering after an insult.
She repeated stories of injury, teaching me to exact
a degree of revenge. If someone called her *hillbilly*
or a bitch, God help them, she would light a cigarette
and exhale smoke and smile like God was on her side,
knowing that what she did next would make a great story.
My favorite for a long time involved a new-car salesman
telling my mother she would need a husband's signature
on a loan application. She said she set the man straight
not by showing her swell legs or batting her eye lashes
but with phrases like *I'm the one making the payments*
and *I'd like to buy that red Ford if you'd care to sell it.*
If you were the child of divorced parents, you were tainted.
Other kids couldn't play with you because you were different.
I kept a cool head as I fought my way home from the bus stop
because I knew my mother would want to hear about my day.
She'd want the truth and I wouldn't lie. I'd narrate, precisely,
telling my own story of crisis and character assassination.
She quizzed me, daily, and I learned to distinguish cruelty
from stupid remark. It was like there was a war going on
for the hearts and minds of all of us, kids and adults alike,
and she was teaching me which open limousines to avoid
riding around in. I knew her truth wasn't the whole truth,
that you take a beating, regardless, but she was my mother.
I listened, hanging on every bullet of a word she let fly.

## Zombie Apocalypse

In the halls of the nursing home the resident-patients
zombie forth. A woman named Dorothy sentinels a door,
a key-code locked white door. She's looking for her chance.
In hospital slippers, Dorothy affects her best prison stare—
but I'm past her and beside my mother in a few strides.
Mother is five-eleven. One-thirty-seven. She's thin.
I hand her a box she opens with help. Chocolates.

When she finishes, she closes the box. Hands it back.
Asks, *Why are you here, Billy?* I'm not Billy. A nurse
says she's been striking attendants. Kicking, hitting
other residents. Around every exhausted official word
a wheel of better times spins, though it's slowing down.
I say, *I'm sorry to hear that* and take my mother's arm.
And consider killing her—I carry a knife on my belt—

but movie-butchery is R-rated for a reason: the gore.
There'd be blood. I'd think of roses, Mother's Day.
But then I'd have the memory of her fear as elegy.
Dorothy is beside us, telling my mother the world
is ending. For them, it is. And the three of us walk.
Dorothy loses interest in endings, and my mother
changes the subject. There is always that to do.

## The Bones of Appalachia

A friend of mine from Wise, Virginia
tells me, "You are one of us, we together,
the bones of Appalachia as the meat rots."
He says it knowing that both my parents
despise the rough country they come from
and live in what he calls "the literal world"
after leaving home and Neon, Kentucky.
He knows they say I'm not an Appalachian.
My friend was eighteen when David Walters
told him of Sin, the need to be born again.
He may not have known much of heaven
but he knew about things needing changed.
Says he went forward and accepted Jesus
"in some Jesse Stuart mirage of yesteryear
that never was." So he got redeemed, saved.
What Jack Wright swallowed, I swallowed.
Same savior. Same threats of hellfire and
same robber-baron Christianity as history.
Same stupid belief that want and poverty
are to be endured. Lies of that magnitude
burn like moonshine. Stink like a meth lab.
These days, neither of us believes in heaven.
If there is a joy after death for Appalachians,
it's in the springing back of trampled grasses.
Jack says he remembers mountain women
tottering to church in lace shoulder-shawls,
reeking of Este Lauder or morning toddies,
a few sporting bruises saved up from men
who literally hated the world. These dead
sleep now, if death is anything like sleep,
all the theologies of redemption put to rest,
under the pearling snows. Their bones are
in the hills they loved and hated to leave
if they had to, even to save themselves.

## Drinking from the Colored Only Drinking Fountain

I don't tell this to make fun of the South
or to diminish the awful suffering of others
but because I want always to be this Roy.
It would've been my first trip to Florida.
Before air conditioning. I would've been 5
maybe 6, Elvis on the radio and segregation
in place in the US of A. The scallop-edged
glossy black-and-white photographs that
survive from the trip are each stamped '59.
I was big for my age. In the photographs
I've got a gut. A chubby kid, even then.
Buddha-bellied. A little Yankee twerp.
My mother Nettie hovered, her hand
in my hand, most of the time, but once
in a public park somewhere in Tampa
I must've given her the slip and gone
rogue. Because they, both my parents,
tell a story of Little Roy—they used to
call me that or Roy Glenn—getting in
line for one fountain but then noticing
that a perfectly-good Other Fountain
had no one near it. They say I scooted
off to step on the brass governor-pedal
at the base of the ancient contraption
and get a spring-fed-and-teeth-chilling
mouthful of water intended for Coloreds.
I may have lacked a capacity for grace
or athleticism, but I was smart enough
to know water's water, and to wave off
shouts to the contrary and get me some.

## Strange Privacies

*If you believe an afternoon can collapse*
*into strange privacies—*

—Stephen Dunn, "Welcome"

My cousin who knows like Scripture
the universal need for rescue
says his father had a '60 Imperial
fall on him in a garage in Ohio.
My cousin who heard God's voice
(he claims) pronounce the word *Missouri*,
thinks his father's far-off voice
from beneath the white Imperial
filled those same unfillable spaces of self
when he keened, "Get help, son!"
My cousin who could not leave
his unfortunate, trapped father's side
at the bottom of a cloud made of dust
and thirdhand-because-it's-what-you-have
faulty jack-stands found himself running
into a house his mother had just left.
My uncle was a cruel man, and feared.
But pinned under the full weight
of his bum luck, he must have sounded
small and human. A man who took pride
in having never prayed. Until the dead
heft of his prize rust-bucket thudded
down through a gauze of electric light
onto his unprotected chest and tattooed
left arm. When they got the car off,
he was a better man, better father,
for a day or two. Years later, my cousin
sold his trailer and household goods
to answer a voice at about the decibel level
of a weak whisper. He went, he said,
because of who it was. Which meant
he thought the asking might go on and on.

## The National Cash Register Company Christmas Tree

Even if the tree is only the consequence of an invention based
on a contrivance to track and record rotations of a ship's propeller,
it's Christmas Eve. My cousins Jim and Bob are in the Ford
—a '64 Galaxie 500, flame-red with white sidewall tires—
their mother is riding shotgun. We're part of a line of cars
appraising the mammoth Norway spruce rainbowing every
blinking color of the spectrum. And my mother is driving.
She's thirty-one, her sister Peggy a year or two younger.
Her favorite sister reaches to dust ash from a filter cigarette.
Each woman is a toned-down version of Loretta Lynn—
big hair, lipstick as red as the hood and fenders of the Ford.
Both have jobs in factories, our fathers / their husbands gone.
Bob has pinched Jim, and my aunt has to turn and pronounce
*Bobby Ramsdail!* in a voice edged with threat then forgiveness.
She reminds him Santa is coming to bring his Western outfit.
Peggy and my mother know about disappointment. Poverty.
They tune the radio to "Rudolph the Red-nosed Reindeer".
The excess of the NCR tree may trump a carload of hope,
still it's nice to trust union wages and sing. And we do—
Bob too—the windshield of the Galaxie 500 wreathed
in the most fervent light the five of us may ever see.

## 2808 Comanche Drive, Kettering, Ohio

After my mother robbed the Shell station,
two Kettering policemen came to our house
to let her know that technically it wasn't *really*
a robbery since her husband owned the business.
But they'd been called. Had some questions.
Summer was mostly over, shafts of sunlight
falling at the feet of the standing policemen
until she offered them coffee and they sat,
accepting cups, cream and sugar. Hearing
of her abandonment. Shifting their holsters,
their cop gizmory, and calling her *ma'am*.
The thinner man opened a spiral notebook.
Clicked a ballpoint pen and started writing.
Mother was a beautiful woman then. Gutsy,
and more than a match for the world of men.
Time passed. There was laughing. They left.
She emptied an IGA bag, a brown grocery sack.
Looked around the room, checking on an infant
and a toddler, my sisters, smiling and cooing as
she started counting loose bills, stacking them
on the table where the cops had left their cups.
She reconstructed for me, for herself, the look
on the face of the man with a name-tag egg
reading *Bob* who'd emptied the cash drawer.
In some lightning-flash dendrite of memory
preserving the shared struggle of our life then,
I can see her unfold and smooth ones fives tens,
waving and pocketing the occasional twenty,
shoving my way a mostly-silver sea of coins,
saying, *Here, count* because she could and
because her face burned, red-hot, with an
end-of-summer light and something else.

## Yankee Pride

All that winter Jerry Hagerman had talked Jesus, quoting Scripture.
Smoke for which there was no ceremony or language hung in the air.
The smoke, now that I think of it, might have been the cigarette fires
in the ashtray of his '60 Oldsmobile. Then he went home to Delaware
and came back with two jars of clear liquid. Yankee pride, he called it.
Rested the jars on a kitchen table. *This is Daddy's first since they let him
out of the penitentiary. First through new copper.* I was maybe 14, a kid,
trusting a pomade-in-the-hair ex-football star from Delaware who knew
at least a part of the raucous truth of the world, having been in the Army.
Born-again Jerry got a kick out of pouring me a tumbler. Saying, *Drink it.*

That day, I learned every scalding atom of it has a grudge against the body.
I didn't smell it. I downed it like 7UP. One greedy mouthful, trusting Jerry
who said he put his trust in the red-lettered passages of the New Testament.
When couples groove on a dance floor, nasty-dancing like Bacchic initiates,
acolytes performing their duties in a temple of tail-chasing, it's moonshine
that has them up, doing the Dirty Boogie. Oh, I puked. Through my nose,
dry-heaving again and again with the force of a simple prayer for absolution
until the American Standard toilet god was satisfiedI'd sacrificed enough.
That whisky burned like Perdition flames. If you believe there's a Perdition.
If you believe what Jerry did. If you swallow some, all, or any part of it.

## Starlight Taxi

I'm the Good Son who stood at his bedside
with the wad of paper towels for the blood,

and for the last applause of his ruined lungs.
He may have suffered before falling back

and a crown of thorns of sweat beads paraded
across the window filling with the hospital bed

and him, my father, in a white J.C. Penney t-shirt
stitched to start of night. You could say his death,

the track of it, included one sequin-pearl of spit
at mouth's edge, a blushing star whose shit job

was to transport that aggregate of light and dark
to wherever it, they, go after moments like that.

You could say his settled face acquired a pallor
pinned to the flesh, a look of winded surrender

part fear of not being in the world, part release,
the eyes suddenly the color of dry-ice smoke.

## Why William Earl "Bill" Hagerman Carried the Casket

First, because he asked. Because he loved my mother.
Never mind that he was high. And not *just* high but staggering.
At the viewing at the funeral home. And then at the funeral.
I've been that impaired on you-name-it drugs and alcohol.
And for a lot of years. Let's just say, I knew the signs.

But I was at my mother's funeral, hearing for the third time
how my drug-addled cousin should be one of the pallbearers.
Over my daughter and my sons and a cousin my mother adored
like a son. Or in place of my father who had the strength then.
This is my mother we're talking about. Not one of those mothers
who proffer kisses at Easter and Christmas and graduations
but keep their bank balances a secret. A practitioner of the art
of unconditional love. And I was sitting before her casket,
looking at the silver cross on the inside of the raised lid—
a shiny token pinned to the lining and hovering over her.

A roomful of men and women had been brought there
from far away, like my mother's coffin, by Eisenhower's
Interstate System to be put to use then promptly forgotten.
So I understood wanting to keep something for yourself.
I thought, *Let he who is without sin cast the first stone.*
Something she might quote then smile as if to say, We've
all been there. I got up. He was crying. The front of his shirt
was wet. I said, I know you're high, Bill. Don't drop her.
I told him he'd take my place. And we shook hands.

Cut to the cemetery. It had rained and the way to the grave
was soft, so he stepped on the foot of another pallbearer
who caught himself and more than his share of the weight—
turns out, some know to do that—so they didn't drop her.
And I'll always have my own stepping aside at the grief
of another. Which is what she knew to do. And taught.

## Hillbilly Poems

Here's how full of self-loathing Appalachians are:
my mother said once there was no way I was one,
a hillbilly, since I'd attended college, and graduated.
She used words like 'articulate' and 'equivocation'—
which was her way of saying, without equivocation,
that everyone she knew from the hills was a dumbass.
Any poem about hillfolks assumes that self-loathing.

Then, because there is violence and suicide, adultery
and betrayal at large in the world, those will be there.
Proportions may be jacked up a bit by Poverty and
inarticulate despair as cavernous as any coal mine.
Death is in a hillbilly poem, the grieving of a death.
And giving God part of the blame. The poems ask
that He wince at capitulation as much as unbelief.

You could call them prayers, but the music of fiddle
and banjo breathes in each line of free verse or iambic
pentameter to remind you of the scent of wood smoke
and clear river water crooning over moss-slick stones.
In hillbilly poems there is always a break for bluegrass.
A joint to hit and hit again. And a drink of something.
Ancient Age, maybe. Always in pint bottles, though.

The voices of the poems may or may not have accents.
Cadences borrow from the thorough beating of the hills
at the hands of the machinery of mining. They're hymns
to the dives and the dancehall band playing cover tunes,
to six-cylinder or V-eight engines grinding to life again
in midsummer yards where parts cars shake off the dust
of uselessness like a dulcimer in the right, skilled hands.

## A Street of Small Houses

Coma $^{n}$che –that's the way my father wrote it,
in ink, on a gray granite stone retrieved from the
outstretched open palm of the hand of a hill, a cold
at the flesh-edge of things where death asserts itself.
The hill was behind our house on Comanche Drive,
in Ohio, the house we had long since moved from,
where he and my mother had broken one another
and then joined at the breaks and continued on like
a couple of Olympians swimming asynchronous laps
in a pool where the filtered water stirs filtered water.
Maybe he had forgotten how the noun *Comanche*
is spelled in English, but this says what he recalled
after the migratory bird of Reminiscence changed
its course of flight, hard-turning in midair to fly
away from those days in some other direction—
crossing the preternatural thresholds of this life,
refugee from its own linkages to the land and sea,
a mascot of the School of Remembrance, the need
to know again, a two-headed bird homeward bound.
I tried to wash off the writing after he died. But
thought better, wanting to keep a part of the truth.
Maybe shoulder some responsibility for the failure
to love enough that you feel prized. Maybe make
an offering to the everyday that couldn't care less
whether we keep rolling found stones up the hills
of forgiveness or turn them over once in the hand
as explanation, hoping the stories resolve after
a soul and body have waited one another out.
The street had nothing to do with Comanches,
though life in America is all about being moved
from one stretch of good ground to another. Like
my father who walked upright and unrepentant
in the light of Ohio before being swept away.

## Converters

*"In 1946 money answered everything."*

—Philip Levine

In 1974, Walker Manufacturing of Hebron—
a parts supplier for Ford Motor Company—
changed over from making catalytic converters
in the pursuit of a little more breathable air
to making mufflers for the overseas markets
where the EPA isn't charged with the job
of tapping factory owners on the shoulder
to say, *No way are you getting away with that.*
In 1974, money and a good job answered a lot.
Then winter arrived. And from the factory roof
you could have looked down on rows of Fords
(Chryslers and GM cars, too) waiting in the cold.
You could have imagined yourself in heaven
or Ohio—a thousand or so brightly colored cars
and trucks accepting the eucharist of snowfall—
red green blue yellow black hoods budding out
in the lot behind the converter factory. You could
have called down fire to cancel those lay-off slips
falling on the asphalt like pink leaves to transform,
once wet, into a blood-dark litter. Not that far off,
leaving the factory, I could hear the music of Bad
Company. Elton John. Rod Stewart. Gregg Allman.
Music turned up so loud you could hear it above
the roar of engines and gear-shifts. What you didn't
hear was the steady rise and drop of presses, the hiss
of annealers, the *beep!-beep!-beep!* of the forklifts.
In a week I learned the luck of having the GI Bill
and being able to read, able to make a few changes
of my own. Before I knew it I was a college student
listening to the history of whole armies of pioneers
with wagons and picks and shovels, hellbent on going
west to convert a nation of Plains Indians and Nature

to accepting their messianic thinking as God's plan,
a world of separate but unequal which we still call
living in the service of an America undreamed of.
Is this what we were taught? That's the question
that calls out now like a preacher to the heathens.
I promised myself I would move on. And I have.
But if the lay-offs at Walker are a dream fulfilled,
and it isn't my dream, or yours, then whose is it?
What voice deeper than Gregg Allman's, deeper
than the well of common sense and patriotism,
have I failed to hear? And what's my plan now,
now that no songs of protest or joy send chills
up and down my spine? now that I'm too old
and settled in my ways to raise a fist to the sky?
The hardest part isn't losing a job and pausing
to try and figure out your place in a new world.
The hardest part is when someone tells you
about America and defines promise as hope,
and a love for the truth pushes you to give
the raised middle finger to what you hear.
The hardest part is living without hope.

## Famous Blue Raincoat

*Well I see you there with the rose in your teeth*
*One more thin gypsy thief . . .*

—Leonard Cohen, "Famous Blue Raincoat"


The year I first heard Leonard Cohen sing of gypsy thieves
and the sort of loss you dread like conscription, I bought
a black leather motorcycle jacket. I didn't own a motorcycle.
I owned my experience: enlisting to avoid being drafted
and sent to Nam. The jacket was my Famous Blue Raincoat,
a symbol. I'd seen *The Wild One*, and it was that jacket—
the kind with the belt in the back and silver snaps, zippered
sleeves, a design to cover anatomic regions of the upper body
in case of a crash. The first time I wore it and waltzed in
to the Union Bar & Grill in Athens, Ohio, I liked the way
women paid attention to me. I liked the man I was then:
back from the air force, a giant chip on my gypsy shoulder
the size of a country. I drank beer and didn't mind crashing
and burning for the better part of a day afterwards. Some men
are halved by their lives; some women, too. But whatever else
a self is, besides a set of understandings we put on and take off
like this year's fashion or a uniform, in the jacket I felt whole.
I was building myself from a kit, and the black leather jacket
was my Cloak of Visibility, you could say: Whatever mystery
surrounds attraction, whatever prayer for peace wearing it was
(the Beatles wore jackets like it, in their early publicity stills,
or John Lennon did) the thing drew women. On top of which
I wore wire-rimmed glasses with tinted lenses (like Lennon)
night or day. They were part resolve, part a promise I made
myself to look past appearances, to scratch the surface for
whatever depth is, even if it's more surface—the way a Plato
or Aristotle might. I think it was Plato who said, *Only the dead*
*have seen the end of war.* I'm not saying I was Marlon Brando,
metaphorically slouching on some iron horse in movie light,
or Plato. I'm saying I was from Ohio and learning to live.

## Hell's One-Walled and Lovely Hanging Garden

*Only so much room,* the man says,
then ushers you through what you judge
to be infinite space. He points out a rabble
jigging in death clothes, asks you
to forgive the jostling and epic stench.

A nexus of footpaths brims with a fecal smell,
the walking new-dead, a plaintive winding flow
bodied mostly by soldiers. Now he gossips

about a crossing-guard priest who laughs
with a brown-shouldered prostitute.
His eyes, bad neighborhoods, turn in
upon themselves like the eyes of the poor.

The place is a panel in a triptych for an empire
of wailing—palisades are a rapture of ruined blossoms,
the walls themselves graffiti-splashed
with spray-painted messages
in Arabic, in English.

Stepwise windows carry the darksome weight
of crypts and mausoleums. Black-winged angels
sentry the ramparts, gripping great stones;
fronds of fern bisect an exclamation point of stairs.

Thousands of fiery blowing ropes
of bloom give off an unfiltered scent:
lavender and sickrooms.
There's much you want to ask
as perimeter flames scroll
before reaching almost to heaven.

## Woman and Alligator

*A Port Charlotte woman hit an alligator
in her Honda Accord and tried to save it.
But she crashed when the 6-foot reptile
began to thrash around in the backseat.
She was charged with possession
of an alligator, a felony in Florida.*

—*Tampa Tribune*

She probably said *Goddammit* and *Motherfuck*
and braked. She says she got out and grappled
with the scaly Crocodilian before she thought.
She'd been singing along with Ashlee Simpson,
but hefting a 6-foot reptile into a Honda says
she was one *big* Floridian. She drove on
with the beast on a beach towel in the back.

When it came to, and bared 80 teeth and whip-
thrashed its squamous tail, woman and alligator
spilled across lanes like a tourist. She stopped
and a Florida State cruiser rolled up. The cop
would have given her a ticket and foregone
the lecture and handcuffs but, no, she had to
start in kicking, swearing at its Zen stillness,

saying she hadn't graduated FSU for this shit.
And what of the gator? They coaxed it out,
tossed a McNugget in the desired direction.
Toward water, away from I-4's roaring stream
of truck traffic. It waddled off, a pretty bad
song about the wreck of postmodern love
running, looping through its reptilian brain.

# V

*from* Walking with Eve
in the Beloved City

## *"Robert Plant Holding a Dove That Flew into His Hands, Circa 1973"*

—*photograph from the concert at Kezar Stadium*
San Francisco, June 2, 1973

The wing-flutter resolves like a breath of fog
by San Francisco Bay. Like sand or white sails.
This year, every snapshot of Robert Plant onstage
describes the outline and contour of his cock
through jeans. This is that. But the heart inside
the successful crooner is what it is: Frank Sinatra
with a smidgen of Elvis tossed in for good measure:

Shelley's Adonais resurrected with a mane of hair
and management, a record deal and Jimmy Page.
Now the fingers tipped with nicotine gesture
to the starveling crowd about to feast—
the hand dealing with both a lit Marlboro
and a bottle of English beer. Which is when
the rock dove lands on the other hand. Settles

like news of the death of Keats settled on Shelley.
This congregation still wants directions to Paradise
if not ushered to the stairs. Taught the shibboleth
for entry. What it gets is the flight of the dove,
impromptu cooing, the talons ringing fingers
as if what we call beautiful is straightening
the curve of its spine and starting to sing.

## Our Local Heavens

Roy-the-father hands Roy-the-son the Testor's glue.
Says, *Go easy* as he soliloquizes about the engine,
saying that the 265-horsepower unsupercharged dual
overhead cam four-valves-per-cylinder automobile
was the most expensive most powerful Straight-8
built in Des Moines, Iowa or anywhere in those days.
Roy-the-father tosses out "built entirely by hand,"
which is printed on the Monogram box. He shows
how $1/32^{nd}$ scale pieces dry-fit. Says the Model J
is like a Duesy the movie-version Daisy Buchanan
raced over Myrtle Wilson with in *The Great Gatsby.*
Roy-the-son doesn't know then that Roy-the-father
has the date of the novel wrong, the model mixed up.
Roy-the-son is inventing scenarios whereby the vehicle
raises rooster tails of red dirt, a captain of industry or king
or Hollywood film star at the wheel and driving far too fast.
Which is how this ends, building the Duesenberg—the model
doused and set alight, its chimeric canary-gold plastic melting,
Roy-the-father having exited Roy-the-son's life, a son's stock
of enchanted objects decreased, the count diminished by one,
as Gatsby's was after the green light on Daisy's dock dimmed.
Tonight, the local heavens of the room smell of Testor's glue.
Roy-the-son is still a boy and still nuts about Roy-the-father.
The tricky cement is hardening as it should. Not too quickly
since model building is the chance for a father to tell a story
whose end isn't predicated on a knowledge of good and evil
or understanding what fathers owe sons without knowing it.
Disaster is everywhere. Yet, for now, most of that is outside.
In here, chrome-trimmed running boards reflect dreamlight.
Roy-the-son grasps the Duesy and makes a flying motion.

## How Not to Spell Gymnasium

*for Al Maginnes*

As for the rest, they spat consonants and vowels
in correct order while I was in the john
and so not around when the Bs were called,
my phonological bowels a reproach to thoughts
of metalinguistic glory. I wanted an easy one:
*Diarrhea: d-i-a-r-r-h-e-a. Diarrhea.*
Like all of my life to come, I wanted
what I wanted and got what I was handed
instead. Most children like language—
they breathe near-painful meaning, kids,
and they look you dead in the eyes
until they forget—as I did—or look away
and dash to error. Shame. For the rest
of my life I'd recall what being in a hurry
gets you: asked to have a seat at a desk
of carved-and-initialed mutable moments.
All right, so I spat a *j* first fucking thing
and had to play-act at being glad for others
while being taught a valuable lesson: not
to be looking at Shelley Staddon's budding
breasts; as if I could stop myself, as if, like Jesus
who, on the Cross, learned about phonemes
blending and segmenting—what's the Aramaic
for sacrifice—and that loss decants too easily
from us, like Jesus, like that *j* instead of *g*,
spewed while thinking of acrobatic *c-l-o-u-d-s*
above the gray-shiny slide and a Jungle Jim—
there was that resurrectionist of a *j*, which
had tricked me into thinking there is no trick,
that once you understand the future has breasts—
*Breasts: b-r-e-a-s-t-s*—you watch your step down
from Rolling Fields Elementary School's stage
past what is beyond words, thinking you know
a way to move through the life you're given.

# 1975

*Once upon a time you dressed so fine*
*You threw the bums a dime in your prime, didn't you?*

—Bob Dylan, "Like a Rolling Stone"

My girlfriend Sherry asks why Lindsey Buckingham
is so thin as she cradles the album *Buckingham Nicks*.
This is before he and Stevie Nicks join Fleetwood Mac.
I tell her he's a rock star and that rock stars are ghosts.
A turntable spins. The small apartment smells of sex,
marijuana. Most of one wall is an *Easy Rider* poster.
Fonda and Hopper on Harley choppers. In a corner
of the poster a DISCOVER AMERICA sticker.

Saigon is falling. Sherry shows me a *Newsweek*—
pages of color photographs of helicopters, sailors
shoving them from the deck of the *USS Okinawa*
into the South China Sea, chopper blades nicking
the rough waters of the Pacific, spinning to a stop
on a turntable-axis of collective national disgrace.
She points to the regimental insignia and US flag.
I rise and stagger to the turntable. Lift the needle.

I know what she wants: any album by Bob Dylan
where two lovers are the A-plus-B in a mathematics
of fulfillment-for-a-little-while, that equation solved
though the republics of the sad earth slide into collapse,
ruin, refugees crowding onto last ships where the deck air
reeks of diesel and human sweat and a blue transistor radio
blares: *I see your hair is burnin' / Hills are filled with fire*
*If they say I never loved you / You know they are a liar.*

# Walking with Eve in the Loved City

## 1. John and George Wore Matching Black Swim Trunks

> *"We settled in the Key Wester hotel. For a few hours, on September 10th, the boys relaxed. John waded into a swimming pool with several members of the Exciters, a '60s pop group—3 girls, 1 guy, all African-American. The pictures of John in the pool with black women enraged Southern reporters. The photos became an overnight sensation."*
>
> —Larry Kane

This is 1964. After a photo-shoot for LIFE magazine
where 3 black women lollygag in the swimming pool
at the Key Wester with John Lennon. At poolside,
they aren't raising their middle finger to the South.
They don't see it that way. They're negotiating,
by phone, the segregated seating at the Gator Bowl.
They won't perform. Meaning there is right and fair
and this isn't that. George Paul Ringo kid reporters.
They're doing what good lads have always done: Talk

women. And no one wants Lennon interviewed. No one
wants a bloody scuffle like at the clubs in Hamburg. They
want Johnny writing hit songs to *buy* hotel swimming pools.
They blame scheduling. And the hurricane. And then perform,
the show like thread leading back to the matching swim trunks.
Across Florida, in St. Augustine, a white motel owner-operator
splashes muriatic acid into a pool where blacks are swimming.
The photograph makes Jimmy Brock as notable as the Beatles
in water where the past is light and drags everything with it.

## 2. How Barbie and Ken Wound Up
on The Daily Show with Jon Stewart

*"If Barbie is so popular, why do you have to buy her friends?"*

—Steven Wright

Bored with being dolls, they wanted to give breath
and flesh to approximate lusts. Give motion a try.
When the laptop screensaver was the only light,
they sloughed the definitions of non-Existence.
Ken made a move and Barbie answered, stroking
his Interesting Place with its suggestion of genitalia.
She had absolutely no idea there were others watching.
Still, she wasn't unhappy when it wound up on YouTube.
They didn't intend to upstage Arnold Schwarzenegger or

Congressman Weiner or that IMF banker who'd assaulted
hotel maids when he wasn't working to loot the Free World.
They didn't see themselves as circus freaks, Ken and Barbie,
but there was the matter of fame. And what *is* an icon to do?
Of course Stewart's people broke out dollhouse patio furniture,
as if the only response to Barbie Millicent Roberts and cohort
was walk-on music by the Beach Boys and spinning vortices
of red and white and blue. Stewart: *Do comparisons between
dollhood and the Frankenstein monster ever bother you two?*

### 3. Walking with Eve in the Loved City

*"And the loved city? Only at a distance can it be loved."*

—Mark Jarman

Since all things are present at the same time in one place,
and since that place has a name we translate as *paradise*,
she dangled before me in a first-language of crucifixes.
Her eyes appraised me like a sale rack. The look said
that it would be getting dark forever somewhere soon.
I figured she had the keys to the kingdom or a Bentley
parked like a prophecy up the road in the moonlight.
Clearly, she was unhappy. I guessed Adam was off
inventing pari-mutuel off track betting or the trifecta.

There were angels. Some with red-white-and-blue wings.
And Eve asked me if a black angel was subject to searches
that a white angel wasn't. I reminded her where we were.
I didn't want tagged for staring—she was a knock-out—
and so I looked off at a robed man who was bending low
to talk Pashto to a predator part lion part Nile crocodile.
"I'm not afraid of this thing," he said, straightening up.
He reached to pet the lion-croc. Turned. Stared at me.
Then: "I'm more afraid of Americans, aren't you?"

## Jeff Goldblum in The Fly

When he gets Geena Davis into his laboratory,
she winds up taking off a black silk stocking.
A reporter, there for the Story, she rolls the
stocking down her thigh then knee then calf,
as if the mixing of business and pleasure goes
with the territory. Something she knows about.
She steps out of her stocking. Hands it to him,
smiling. And he dissolves and rematerializes it.

White people shouldn't mix with black silk stockings,
or mix them with science. They can't handle it. Cut
to her taking the story to her editor who calls Jeff
Goldblum / Seth Brundle a con man. A magician.
Cut to the lab: a baboon in a telepod, the animal
zapped to become—yuk!—a squirming mass.
Red-goo monkey steak but alive and in pain.

Seth then pontificates about the poetry of flesh.
He says the computer translates or *mis*translates
what it supposes flesh to be. Says the problem
is the computer can only repeat an impression
of a baboon. Which is his and isn't even close.
No understanding of Poetry yields no monkey
reassembled in approximately correct fashion.

They kiss—she kisses him—they fall together.
After a breakthrough revelation about the body,
a next baboon bounds out intact. Monkey see,
monkey do: Seth goes next, the stowaway fly
on the window of the teleporter his undoing.
What is science if not poetry translated? Of
course the experiment turns to shit. (It's love,
why wouldn't it?) Seth starts to crave sugar
and fuck like Superman on steroids. Lectures
about wanting to *really* penetrate the flesh.

He's buzzing now. To think, it all started with the best intentions. And love, which we hope will absolve us of everything.

# Fitzgerald and Zelda, February 1921

> *"All good writing is swimming under water*
> *and holding your breath."*
>
> —F. Scott Fitzgerald

In the photograph, Zelda wears a fur and hat.
Scott has on a top coat and gloves. It's winter.
He said Zelda had "an eternally kissable mouth."
Said that he loved stories of her in Montgomery.
He'd begin: *Montgomery had telephones in 1910.*
*It's April. A warm day. Magnolias are blooming.*
*Zelda—ten years old—has rung up the operator*

*to dispatch the fire department. She climbs out*
*onto a roof to wait rescue. Lots of white blossoms*
*are falling on small shoulders. Landing in her hair.*
*She's sitting, smoothing her dress when they come.*
Whatever else, they looked swell in photographs.
He'd say, *Zelda drew flyers from Camp Sheridan*
*who did figure-eights over her Montgomery home.*

*They crashed their biplanes trying to impress her.*
What he would never say: Then she married me.
As if what happened to her later was his fault
or a series of regrets for which he was to blame.
In 1921, each existed to watch the other move—
*This Side of Paradise* was a hit, he was soaring.
Zelda wanted to soar herself. Float like a ballerina.

At the end of the day she wanted what she wanted:
a ticket out of Alabama. Excitement. Breathlessness.
After her third breakdown, the years in sanitariums,
visitors whispered, *She was a beauty once.* Trapped
at last in a burning asylum, the fire real, Zelda Sayre
Fitzgerald died locked in. Screaming to be rescued.
He would've been dead, buried, for years by then.

## Saturday Afternoon at The Midland Theatre in Newark, Ohio

Slouched in a theater seat and watching *Bullitt* for the third time, a look I get from an usher might best be described as granting a general amnesty and full pardon for my having shelled out only the one admission price. There's the balcony with its blue and red curved seat backs. By a door to the upstairs men's room a framed likeness of the Civil War drummer boy, Johnny Clem, whose baby-faced looks and sudden-dark hair remind me of a young Italian, then Sal Mineo in *Rebel Without a Cause*. There's that angels-in-the-architecture grand gesture of a ceiling, the wall of drapes of eloquently pleated purple. And there's the screen framed in its filigree of gold and silver. The usher is accommodating me by simply not noticing—I'm on my third popcorn, third enormous Coca-Cola, second box of Milk Duds, when I realize I'm happy. Elated. In Ohio at fourteen you're disappointed most of the time. So I want to tell Frank Bullitt just how it feels to be from Dayton and new here, a fat-kid eighth grader at Fulton Middle School. But then, Steve McQueen is French-kissing Jacqueline Bisset good-morning. Strapping on a shoulder holster and .38 pistol. Now he's stopped at the corner of Clay and Taylor, searching the pockets of his trench coat / suit coat for change. I've loved that look all afternoon. The usher reacts as if that says it, that fuck-the-world expression of Frank Bullitt as he gives up and bangs the cover and steals a newspaper. Turns out, 1968 isn't for the faint of heart. You need a Mustang GT 390. Ice water for a blood type. A tolerance for the visages of the dead you made dead, slaughtering out of that old American purity of motive that dissolves into a communion of terrific car chases wherein thunderous algorithms of horsepower rule.

## Whatever Else, This Memory Resembles a Dance

My earliest recollection of my grandmother Potter involves a warning.
It was about certain terpsichorean behavior: *No Dancing on the Sabbath.*
This would've been before we moved to the brick house in Kettering.
I only know it stuck and became That Which Is Older Than Memory,
a word-for-word Eleventh Commandment she authored then forgot.
It was as if we were together in a House of Ten Thousand Candles,
she and I, and she'd issued an exhortation to steer clear of matches,
then was jolted by a love of fire and brightness. Maybe I made it up.
Either way, I'd say to her *Granny, remember when I was a small boy*

*and you told me never to dance on Sundays?* She'd say, "No, Roy,
I don't remember that." If forgetting is older than history, older than
original sin, then so is making shit up. Meaning, I can't say for sure.
Maybe a doctrine against dance never actually issued from her mouth,
though it's exactly the kind of directive she was inclined to spew forth.
My mother challenges a memory I have of Sonny and Bobby Osborne
playing music in our house on Comanche. In those days, she worked
with the guitar player's girlfriend May. May lived with us in the house
on that low hill. My parents had just divorced, and Benny Birchfield

had dragged the bluegrass duo from Kentucky to Ohio. I remember
Granny coming out of her bedroom in a housecoat. She was in a huff.
I recall her telling them *Quiet down!* and hearing *Sorry, Miss Potter.*
But if Groucho Marx didn't have a duck that dropped from the ceiling
with the secret word, then I didn't hear a prohibition against Sabbath
dancing and the Osborne Brothers and Benny Birchfield never played
in our kitchen, my Granny waiting in the anarchy of light at the edges
of seeing, standing like God (no fan of banjo and Appalachian fiddle)
or Moses in the doorway. About to call it a night and throw them out.

# The Silence of the Belt When It Is Not Striking the Child

—Billy Collins, "Silence"

I had been laughing at my mother, and she did not like
being laughed at, especially by a son who saw his father
stealing the plates from her Olds on his way out the door
as cause for sniggering. The problem was, I couldn't stop.
Tides of out-of-body delight kept bubbling up. Breaking.
Until she left the room. Returned having rescued a belt
he'd abandoned in his hurried rush to be done with us.
We were in the kitchen. And I remember backing up
to the refrigerator. Begging for mercy. Forgiveness.
Her voice rose and fell as she tracked me to strike.
My legs arms back burned. The palm of one hand.
I had never been so utterly shamed. So humiliated.
I'd pissed myself, I saw after as she jerked me up
from a black tile floor saying, *Laugh some more.*

Maybe I have no call to show her in that light.
We had a lithograph of the Blue Boy on a wall.
The den had a gray sectional sofa. A color tv.
In the kitchen cabinet were Oreos. Pop-Tarts.
Outside, an Olds that wasn't going anywhere.
Don't act as if you haven't seen such houses.
Haven't lived on an analogous street where
familiar torments were enacted. Fifty years
have ticked by. And I recall sliding down
the side of our Westinghouse refrigerator,
a boy-cheek compelled to the cool metal
as I asked to be permitted to live a while.
How could I know she wouldn't kill me?
Hadn't I just witnessed the end of love?

113

## Can't Help Falling in Love

We're parked under luminous eaves of aluminum
& it's a summer night & the driver's-side window
is rolled down on my father's '57 Ford Ranchero.
The car-hop has brought us hamburgers & Cokes
& rested a tray under a Seeburg speaker playing
an Elvis Presley song. The car-hop hangs around
like she can't imagine (or doesn't care) my father
is married. Sure enough, he leans out to touch her
on the arm & hand. A nametag reads *Georgia*.

Georgia the Car-hop looks a lot like my mother
if my mother were a waitress at the Parkmoor
on Woodman Drive & had movie-star breasts
& piled-up Dolly Parton big hair & a uniform
that is itself a way of speaking. She leans down,
says something & Ohio is a little more like heaven.

Miss Rocket Tits is talking through the window.
I answer her between bites of my cheeseburger
& a choking swallow of soft drink. I tell her
my name & that it's the same as his—*Roy*—
& she laughs like she's been told (& knows)
a wonderful secret. She asks how old I am
& I have to think & not look at all (I'll stare)
at her bending over in her uniform. Her eyes
sparkle & one of my molded-plastic army men

digs into me from a place in my pants pocket.
I feel my heart beat & beat like the tell-tale one
under the floor in the Poe story I've already read
& had nightmares about. I say "8" & Georgia
smiles, leaves us the check & a wink my father
has to see (but maybe he doesn't), reaching out
into a night stamping its features on the blank
of our lives, his face a template for everything
that shines like Elvis Presley's movie-star hair,
the chrome on a waxed-to-perfection Ford truck.

## The Force of Right Words

You could say the lie was a story about what didn't happen.
Not the tale of my falling and snapping the plastic stock
of a friend's Christmas-gift toy rifle. I told it,
the stretcher, to his mother. And didn't hesitate,
having schooled Wes, the friend, to nod and say nothing.
She had questions. And her line of interrogation was laced
with threat. The Cuban Missile Crisis had shaken us that year.
Kids had developed the habit of looking skyward in dread
and anticipation much of the time they played outdoors.
I saw that sky in the look on the face of Bernie Vines,
Wes' mother. The light of All-Things-American, too.
Some are born to lying. I was a natural—angel-faced,
a few whisper-touch brushstrokes of Frightened Boy—
the sort of kid aware which details work. In what order.
Shared truth does exist, I discovered, but is contingent
upon its utterance not sounding like a scratched LP,
not repeating what the hearer expects to glide through.
It seems a lie can clear the air of a quantity of truth
after which a friend's trusting mother will accept
the hypothetical presence of rowdy older boys,
lanky representatives of the Likely and Possible
descended out of nowhere like crows to carrion.
Marauders from elsewhere. Adolescent thugs
coveting a replica-by-Mattel Winchester rifle.
Bernie bought my story until she got Wes alone.
When she stormed across a shared sideyard
to enlighten my mother, she wasn't smiling.
But then she was. Bernie Vines was a nurse.
A veteran of the day-to-day and hour-to-hour
earthly realities of What's True Most of the Time,
minus the fine gold pixie dust we toss about for luck.
But I'd somehow shown that her austere morality
and principled moment can extend outward as it
bends. Like a length of plastic before it snaps.
The smile was that part of a clear blue Ohio sky
unfilled by Doom, untrafficked yet by missiles.

*Ringo Starr Answers Questions on Larry King Live
About the Death of George Harrison*

First, Larry King mistakenly calls Ringo
*George* then asks him whether his passing,
George's, was expected. He answers that it was.
Says they knew he was sick. Had lung cancer.
I'm watching, though it's none of my business
how grief-stricken Ringo Starr was and likely
still is or whether he was there, at the bedside,
at the moment George left his life for some other,
if you can believe what George believed, which
was that we keep coming back till we get it right.
And when Ringo is about to let down his guard
and be a bit more self-disclosing, even honest,
Larry interrupts, asking, *Do you ever want to
pinch yourself?* And Ringo Starr says, Sure.
In 1988, years before, in another interview,
with George, this years after Lennon's death,
Ringo confessed that he was the poorest Beatle
then laughed and blew cigarette smoke upward.
Which must've seemed terribly funny to George,
an inside joke, because he said *Hello, John* to
the smoke like it was Lennon (by virtue of his
acknowledged wealth) or some spirit he used to
conquer worlds with. Ringo says he was shocked
upon hearing the news of the death of John Lennon,
but that George's death was another thing entirely.
He doesn't quote from the Bhagavad Gita, but it's
as if he wants to say we continue on, are these *spirits*,
a sort of outrageous bliss even to think it, dumb luck
on the order of being hired as the Beatles' drummer.
Maybe he would have said it, with respect to George
or ventured his own beliefs, if Larry hadn't butted in
to ask him which of the Beatles was the best musician.
*You mean, now?* And I want to laugh now because

maybe Ringo's imagining how hard it is to move
your hands after you're dead, or to move at all,
and how impossible it must be to keep time
and tempo in all that anonymous blankness,
the dark become your most imploring fan.

## The Dark Knight, On His Day Off

As Bruce Wayne, he's practicing kicks in the backyard.
Blue-black shadows fall on an oak he batters to let it out—
all that fury and frustration at being so unsuper and a hero.

He's mindful there are paparazzi everywhere with cameras.
Eavesdropping on him. Spying. But he needs not to feel this.
Like he might want to take a life with one blow. Champions

don't behave like that. They kick old oaks until they're sore.
Maintaining the opinion others are worthy—that's the trick.
He recalls first battles. Against teens, really. Besting them

on a fire escape. Having to worry and catch an offender
as he went over. Ordering himself to reach for an ankle
and hold on. Which he did, lowering the sniveling kid

with a gentleness and concern the world shows no one.
He remembers the wrath of bystanders, and answering.
Seventy-eight acts of assault in the first five weeks. No

wonder the citizenry was slow to warm to his methods.
Schooled in morality and machine-gun fire, the noise
fists make stopping an aggressor in stride, so what

if he exists, in no small measure, because he's rich.
Rich guys with a conscience just kick ass differently.
An iPhone ringtone—"The William Tell Overture"—

says Alfred has prepared dinner. One final roundhouse
before toweling off. Ah, the effort this is! Ah, the hours
needed to win (then win again) the designation Good!

He heads in the direction of a door. Wayne Manor.
Sure, he's exhausted. Ready for a meal. A movie:
A young Marlon Brando standing up to a beating.

## Hellhound

This one lazes about by outcroppings, sniffing
itself as if it could smell anything but brimstone,
heady drifts of Sulphur riding the indifferent day.
An unsolicitous look says the Almighty's minions
can go to—never mind. They say he chased cars
and caught one. No beast this definitively ugly
is also stupid, just distracted by the steady influx.

If there were double-wide trailers on the hillsides,
the hillsides awash in the trash of lives, and one
*really* big billboard for Used Clothing and maybe
a Nissan Ford Toyota Chrysler Chevy on blocks
in a sideyard, you'd swear you were home. Now
a priest bends to fluff a tuft of fur, jumps back
as if bitten. He crosses himself for the reason

that habits are what he has. The dog isn't buying
genuflecting, the kindness. And it lunges at him,
at the hem of his cassock, trying to make a meal
of a being who reads Scripture in a sky's looting
light from the sacristy of the rooms of afternoon.
The mutt's no fan of sacerdotalism. Priestcraft.
His job: to devour whatever sort of thief passes.

A kind of divine judgment is in the dog's chains.
If the escape of the priest is a function of grace,
dumb luck, it is also the case that the animal was
tending to a wound received from rough handling.
Which, without possibility of healing, had festered.
Broken open. And nagged like knowing, to the day,
some exact length of time that constitutes Forever.

## Transcendence

There is the human in the drop-winged angels in El Greco
and the ellipses of youth in a milkmaid's face in Vermeer.

There are the spaces between notes in certain guitar solos
by Carlos Santana or Django Reinhardt in which existence
is reconstituted as bliss, orchestrations of mercurial joy.

There is the locker-room smile on Mickey Mantle's face
in the '56-'57 season, the patter of a titan in the ascendant.

There is the talk of afterlife and deities, the sage expression
of caucasian-Christ-in-the-lighted-frame on church walls
and in funeral homes where the newly grieving delight
at *heaven* showing up on the tongue like a eucharist.

And for the poets there is a blankness before words
to be risen above like Dorothy's tornadic, sepia Kansas
in *The Wizard of Oz*, the way a metaphor in some hands
protects and serves like a pair of regulation ruby slippers,
a humbug behind the curtain of the page the best in us.

Maybe the way a lover looked at you after sex,
in the last soulful glow of arousal and climax,
spoke of an escalator to the stars, the escalator
melting like clocks or that one drop of blood
from a cracked-and-hatching egg of a world
in those paintings by Salvador Dali. Maybe

the only rising we do is out of this body.

## Nosferatu in Florida

Maybe vampires hear an annunciatory trumpet solo.
Maybe they gather at the customary tourist traps
like a blanket of pink flamingos plating a lake
and lake shore by the tens of thousands to drink.
The whole, tacky blood circus is theme-park stuff
and as Disneyesque as lifting the lid on a casket
to flit about sampling the inexhaustible offerings
of O Positive like the Sunday brunch at IHOP.
But if you had a booming, amphitheatrical voice
and had been recently rescued from the grave—
if you wore the republic of the dark like a cape
at Halloween, all bets would be off by the signage
for Paradise Tire & Service, a neon-green royal palm.
Bela Lugosi could materialize on a trailer-park lawn
and the locals would miss it, though lap dogs howled
as kingdoms rose and fell. You could say a kingdom
of fangs glows and drips red by the broken temples
and wide, well-lit aisles of Best Buy and Wal-Mart.
By the shadowed homeless holding up placards
hand-lettered in English, as if the kind-hearted
of the nations of the world spoke one language
and could be counted on to forgive misspellings,
bad syntax that announces one life is never enough.
The resurrection of the body is tough everywhere.
In the Sunshine State, despite eons to shake off loss,
a body carries the added burden of perpetual labor
and cyclical, inescapable debt. The dead know this.

## Unicyclist with UM Umbrella

Say you're driving, idling in rush-hour traffic
and the wind has just shared its best open secret.
Say you've come from signing divorce papers.
The palm fronds, streetside, sag as if burdened.

Someone is navigating between cars, busting ass
to get from point A to B in a hellish downpour.
His slaloming of the stopped lines, on a unicycle,
dismantles the distances in a whoosh of inches.

A rain-diamonded thoroughfare sings of his tire,
the rooster-tailing arc of spray from it. It seems
impossible that there could be anyone so at ease
with what it takes to just press on. Like a surfer

stepped from an ocean that radiates through him.
They say we're electrons. Particles, wavelengths.
Still, it takes a native Floridian to move like this
with a University of Miami parasol as accessory.

## Watching the Night Approach of Tropical Storm Rita

Moonlight, pewter-colored ocean, bougainvillea
and Jupiter Beach resolving into palm shadow,
low notes of wind and a thousand-handed slap
on the Atlantic's rolling plain of dark, our faces
the easy radiance at a double door to a lanai
where you released a cricket earlier that day.
A royal poinciana sways beyond pools of rain,

and our reflected twins in the hurricane glass
look back at us like a species of statue
vanishing and coming together again
at last in the soft vestments of clouds.
A scrim of the usual stars and planets
sparks like the eyes of feral animals
shifting shape in the sky above A1A.

Flapping, red pennants on tall poles—
to warn swimmers, I'm told—say a cargo
of breezes from West Africa, Cape Verde,
has come ashore to tug at all things rooted,
just now, as a crazy few wade a path of water
and cricket song past walls of beach chairs
turning gold against the wild, bright waves.

## Dixie Highway

Here date and coconut palms lean, row upon row,
propped upright by lengths of cut lumber, survivors
of last year's hurricanes, bent but straightening out
beside two-lane A1A, what locals call *Dixie Highway*.
Floridians have come to terms with sand and sand's
ceaseless gypsy blowing. But an ocean isn't a thing
you come to terms with, not ever. The dazzlement
of the waves says that, regardless of our preparation,
water gets what water wants. Date palms opening
in a flash of color isn't a thing to be bargained with,
though the air from off the Atlantic is our history,
an American history, meaning bloody. Wind's story
here is the story of slave ships; of war and huge waste.
*Way down yonder in the land of cotton, old times there are
not forgotten—look away, look away . . .* You know the song.
Here I am making a judgment call about the guilty Rule
of Law that bends in response to the capricious whims
and ocean sounds in the blood and bones of the few
every day in South Florida, here where the rich enter
oblivious and leave this life ecstatic in their good fortune
while the rest drive A1A across Jupiter Island, and dream.
I had parents—poor folks, and proud—I'm not crying
for food like some Sudanese orphan pestered by flies
that swarm around Misfortune like the words of a story.
And I know the universe isn't fair: Roads to and from
all begin, any day, in the country of back-breaking work
and low pay. I know, too, that in December the beach
at Hobe Sound will empty, pennants signaling swim-
at-your-own-risk snapping and flapping like mad—
the same wind that spins out the tow and undertow
washes to shore as light and litter, plastic soda bottles,
kelp-draped, arrived from God only knows how far.

*At the Wheel of the Pilar, Ernest Hemingway*
*Addresses the Breezes Off the Coast of Cuba*

In his booming, amphitheatrical voice, he calls out:
Our Father Who Art in Nada, Nada Be Thy Name.

And if the wingbeats of the gulls are God's answer,
they are also the wingbeats of gulls and only that.

He keeps the .32 Smith & Wesson at his waist.
Loaded and holstered—the gun his father shot

himself with. He says that the heirloom pistol
is for bull sharks. It's June, 1941. And the war

in Europe isn't being staged for this American,
but it beats offering $100 to all comers to box

on the docks: bareknuckled or with the gloves.
In any war, the moon is still the moon and me

like this man up to God knows what for Glory.
Everyone on the island is sleeping in the nude

and with a window open, praying for a breeze.
With a crew and a Thompson submachine gun,

again he patrols the north coast to Cayo Confites.
Again, wafers of moon transubstantiate in waves

scarving the hull in all waters, littoral and pelagic.
Again he wants to sink a U-boat with short-fuse

munitions, hand grenades. Rationed diesel fuel
feeds the 75-horse Chrysler, low engine-echo

unbuilding the dark, encouraging shore birds
to change rooms in their houses by the sea.

## Live Nudes

I watch my Florida friend rake a free hand
through his buzzed-off hair, face full of sunset,
as he tells me about a tittie bar named Love Land.
Call him Jim. Jim stocks paint for Home Depot.
Went to Stetson College on a baseball scholarship.
The dashboard-glow greens a surf of horizon-pink
and Jim's face between sips from a Starbucks cup.
I love those discoveries men make about themselves
not meaning to, catcalls of self-knowledge ripped
from smoke so thick it slices with a swizzle stick.
They may hear themselves become Sonny Corleone
in *The Godfather*, calling women *broads* or worse
and forgetting that respect isn't only about knowing
which new stranger's name to loose while sighing
behind dark-lensed Ray-Bans. Don't get me wrong.
I savor the idea of dioramas of long-hair-tossing
showgirls with veteran hearts, women who couldn't
care less why some men want to nuzzle a dream:
pole-proficient *b-yooties*. Still, I say, No thanks.
Jim nods, says *It figures* and *Your loss, my friend*.
He tells me, in the glow of the dashboard LEDs,
that the women at Love Land are thrilled to death
to be doing what they're doing, naked and soaring
across the stage in a state of entrepreneurial bliss,
glimpsing a clock or plotting their children's future.
But riding like this in his Cadillac, by a restaurant
where neon sails bloom, Jim confesses that nothing
is more fleeting than the pirate smile of a pole-dancer.
Says he slipped an Andy Jackson into a G-string to see
Rapunzel ("El") V trophy legs under a sun-and-moon
ball of mirrors. *Spinning the straw of self into gold—*
he doesn't say it like that, but that's what he means.

# Jim Morrison & The Doors in Miami, 1969

Morrison performs a series of affable pats to a cushion
on a backstage sofa. This, to signal the next woman who
loves without hope. If you sport a stiffy for all Creation,
sooner or later, you take it out. Wave it at butterfingered
fandom. Before the show, a woman makes zipper noises,
emancipates him from the infamous leather pants. Which
he steps out of. Manzarek, the organist, bangs to be let in

and a joke about "organ parts" comes to mind. Morrison
elects to rediscover the orthodoxies of a Marlboro. First,
he thumbs a lighter wheel. Then, a hand positions flame
to the tip-end of the cigarette. Zigzags of smoke become
fog-wreathed rollercoaster curves then gray boutonnieres.
This woman, his Florida guide, is from Ohio. And maybe
Miss Ohio thinks, *What's one more fall between acrobats?*

Jim Morrison isn't looking for a future with a house. Kids.
Membership in Cougar Octagon Optimist Club of Dayton.
Meaning, to him, the Buckeye State might as well be Mars.
He shakes his hair. Certain lighting adores a mane of hair.
This March night, the air is an atomization of discontent.
And so he wonders if some Invisible Man in the Sky,
high above the strongbox that is America, fantasizes

stepping out of Paradise. Maybe needs a little time or
maybe to see if the revenant flesh ever gets to be a bore.
And not just to wheedle a welcome-back trumpet fanfare.
A eucharist of blotter LSD is bringing on the color wheel,
rainbowing the upturned face of the woman holding him.
And he smiles. Generations of dead know that smile
as reminiscent of fire shoveled by envious angels.

## Rimbaud Dying

Most days, she pins an orchid into her black hair.
Extravagant petal-crests of white and a dark trough.
Tonight, no orchid, she leans over the man in the bed
hoping he may linger and she can again collect wages,
fill a draw-stringed bag with gems. Each stone an ocean
of sharp starlight and an East Africa of terrible suffering.
Her small, thin hand in his remains a kindness. Mercy.

Again she offers a thin rawhide to soften his screams.
Places the strap in his mouth. It's his season in hell—
nursed by an inamorata smelling of patchouli. Proof
that comfort, unlike forgiveness, can be conscripted.
Outside, no stars. No tolling bells on midnight streets.
Only the annoying buzz of a fly that will see tomorrow.
She curses at the fly in French as a pain-cry subsides

into a string of Bedouin oaths. When he's gone, fallen
back, she traces the Braille of bite marks in the leather.
The fly loots a flesh-crumb nesting in the bedclothes.
Her eyes fix on the amputation-to-the-knee as elegy.
She knows nothing of Verlaine, the trouble in Paris.
Fluent in French, she recalls the last hours and his
mad ramblings and wishes she'd worn the flower.

## The Nascent Soul Selects a Set of Appalachian Parents

There's this ledge you look over. A railing you lean out from
and stare down at a world of souls like the feeder at Sea World.
And I didn't know a hillbilly from dark matter, a skewered star,
looking down beside a hallelujah gallery of bureaucrat-angels.
My soon-to-be-parents would move from Kentucky to Ohio,
so I wouldn't go hungry as a kid. And I wouldn't have to be
referred to, unfavorably, in comparisons to a coal bucket.
So what if I didn't know my ass from a glass of buttermilk.
So what if I'd lug a Southern accent around like a school bag.

A box of rocks might have had more walking-around sense,
but I was sure that I'd be happy—the way he looked at her
and the way she looked back at him like we'd be all right.
A family. And if it didn't happen this way, it could have.
Who can say that it didn't? I mean, there's all this talk
of a heaven they've gone to now, having left the body.
I'm just saying it works both ways. Or that it should.
I'm saying any given heaven goes by several names.
And one of those is a synonym for *Fleming-Neon*.

## Lee in the Orchard, 1865

This was after Lincoln had walked in Richmond.
It was the first week of April. There were blossoms.
Alone with the old agonies and smoldering new ones,
he may have shoved open the corset of a fence. Tied up
his horse Traveler. And the horse may have whinnied,
the animal noise suspending midair like wood smoke.

Lee may have had to ask, *What are you doing here?*
and answer that very good question as best he could.
He knew that he had to answer Grant if not himself.
He may have walked where the promise of fruition
hung enormously still in some distant midsummer,
his apparitional army matching him step for step.

And though a hard justice had found R. E. Lee,
it was abridged by a blur of yellow jackets. Bees.
Something the heart of a flower requires like light.
Something like drops of rain if the rain had wings.
They had followed blood rivers at Chancellorsville.
Angels of the battlefield, he heard them called once

by a boy-lieutenant in the Army of Northern Virginia.
If he considered what Henry (Light-Horse Harry) Lee
might have done, he told no one. And he neither smiled
nor looked in any direction where his face could be read
or decoded as having caught sight of the end of the world
as he paced under and around a buzzing of tiny live things.

*from* **Body of a Deer**
by a Creek in Summer

## People Who Have Nothing

It's like they've had an epidural to the heart,
those with less than what's needed, those who
feel that awful ache to set want aside for a while—
like someone struggling to speak only good
of the dead who has to search for a word
for *selfish*, a tactful adjective that shines;
and, in doing that bit of magic, confesses

that love, for any human, takes practice.
When we visited eastern Kentucky, drove
from Ohio to the row houses of our family
who had chosen not to follow the exodus north,
I saw Less as the house without a furnace
or serviceable linoleum in the kitchen.
I watched those with nothing make biscuits

of flour and what's at hand. Tasted
how their occultations melted in the mouth.
In winter, a sorrowful splendor of coal smoke
storied the air above row houses in a town where
no one was christened White and yet the place
was named Whitesburg or mud-shiny Neon
which repaid no radiance. In all weather,

want shuffled to a metal folding table
to fashion a hand-rolled cigarette
and smoke and lean back and laugh—
as if life is good if there's enough tobacco
and talk of Reds baseball or a Mason jar
delivered from hand to hand to adulterate
most, if not all, of the smaller infelicities.

## Elegy with a Mountain Doctor Riding Home
## from a Stillbirth

The breach was as challenging to turn as a stubborn horse.
Almost as impossible as deciding not to weep on horseback
because tears freeze. As the Bible explains: a time for crying.
His horse is as black as the centers of a brand-new doll's eyes,
a blue-black like the absence of moonlight on a grove of laurel.

He admired the actions of beasts before the dead child came,
for an animal body, any animal or human, is supple to a point.
This boy arrived as a knapsack of forceps fractures. Dead was
when he conceded, though defeat preceded a pronouncement.
No language for how the glow from a fireplace stirs shadows.

He hears *D.V.* as he passes on his way out. Mounts the horse.
If what we do reveals us, he's one taking rein to keep going.
As from some afterlife, snow thickets breathe gray. Silver.
He rides in a sleep-deprived hallucination in which it drops
into the saddle behind, an apparition talking with a voice

borrowed from the antechamber of a tomb. He rides on.
If he was ever excited by the possibilities, he's deflated now,
recalling arterial flow soaking the mattress in a flood of failure,
the man he had been reminded again what we are at war with
and who is, and isn't, winning. It is either late, or very early.

## Blood Relative

Her name was Susan, and I recall she wore the look
men wear after going to war and returning. My father had it—
like he had seen more than one thing worth turning away from.
Not to mention, his mother staring at nothing in a sanitarium
where they took her after she shot at a man she did her best
to kill but somehow didn't. To be animated and sentient
is sometimes a matter of sitting for hours in a rocker
and thumbing the low hills of flesh of one hand.

That was what she was doing when I asked her
and spat out the name of my grandfather Bob Beach,
my father's DNA-donor-only father, our blood relative.
Why she was where she was and had been for many years.
"Who?" she shot back through her hard mouth, the first sound,
the only sound, she had made since we'd entered the room.
I reached for the water near her. Handed her the glass.
A blue tumbler that beaded droplets of a darker blue.

She took it, the glass. Sat it back down where it had been.
They had brought me to see her. Had no idea I might speak.
And I'm sure they were afraid of what she might say back.
Some lives are irretrievably ruined. Hers was one of those.
Mostly she sat in her rocker. All day, every day. The boy
I was reached for her hands. To stop her hurting herself.
She brushed me aside with the gesture they translated
to say we could leave and not be missed. And then

my father called her Mother. He leaned down—
to stop the incessant rubbing. I can't say why she
didn't knock his hands away, only that she didn't.
If there is a God and justice, it's for those like her.
I was five. I wasn't thinking about God or justice.
And when she did look up, it was into a shadow
on an opposite wall, the blue-on-blue eternity
she may have imagined answers to a name.

## The Spell for Summoning and Ending Rain

### 1. Quiller on Fire

Whether afternoon sprawls out with evening
and whether the body itself is a kind of sheath
for the soul, I don't know—the story is this:
the wind in the wheat and stunted grasses turned
on itself and before he knew it, Quiller Bentley
was cut off from his wife Ellen by an unlovely
wall of flame. If it matters at all now to the history
of Kentucky or two people in for the ride of their lives—
it was like she was anesthetized, the way she moved
toward him, though he tried waving her away.
And, when that failed, running farther into the fire
so she had no choice but to turn and go. By the time
neighbors had her under control and pulled Quiller
from the blaze, my great-grandfather was a glove
of smoke and smoldering flesh. That was the first
shock before he screamed a smoky-throated scream
of recognition he'd been charred, and she ran to him
like she might believe in an afterlife and heaven but
knew it would be some time before she saw him again.
There are pieces of the story that no one tells anymore
and some parts of his last hours only he knows because
she never spoke of it, except to point to photographs
and say how handsome he was before that afternoon.
Whether he tried to tell his wife where he'd buried
the Luzianne coffee can of hundred-dollar bills he
covered over a day or two before, I don't know that.
Whether he was wearing boots, the lace-up kind—
if D.V. and Susan, a son and daughter, were there.
I'd have to say he was exactly what he seemed,
a man who didn't think too far ahead or move
too quickly, even if his life depended on it.

## 2. The World as Horse and Rider

In most of America in the nineteen-twenties
they have a word for the people from Kentucky.
An unflattering name for the sons and daughters
born and raised there or born and departed. The word
has the force of "Dago" or "Wop" if you're Italian,
"nigger" if you're African-American—and so on.
A word this hill-born physician hates and has no use for,
figuring let the name for a people who make do with nothing
summon what is Kentucky from the depths of some hell-on-earth
coal mine or the sunstruck shallows by a creek bank. It would be
better not to have to bring up appellations for *Appalachian*
that are anything but praise for faith in the face of hopelessness.
Humiliation, this one knows, is about subjugating a population.
Calling someone *hillbilly* is a nineteen-twenties sort of wink
at Conscience before murder and then disposing of a body.

The night he rides his mare over a blacksnake, the animal rears.
Fortunately, he doesn't leave the saddle or lose his spectacles.
Doesn't call the horse a "hillbilly nag" or worse, doesn't swear
any kind of oath by heaven. The horse isn't trying to kill him.
Maybe someone else but not this miracle man who accepts
reversal and rides on, apologetic under a Kentucky night sky.
He pats his midnight co-conspirator, calls her by a name
his sister Susan Bentley has given her as if trying to coax,
by the unexplained magic of association, some bright future.

He pauses for a minute in silence, D.V., righting himself
in the saddle and stirrups, feathering reins as Shooting Star
looks down the road for more wriggling snakes, then stares
into the distances of steeply rising hills. The tick of water
moving between mossy stones sounds then is drowned out.
Now a dog's bark signs the way, asking on behalf of its master
Who goes there? as if ready to flash fierce teeth and pounce
or be called by its name and found worthy of a kind word.

### 3. At Some Point the Rider Always Lets the Horse Find Its Own Way

D.V. is no different than any man who holds life and death in his hands
and dismisses the miraculous with words like *plumbing* and *playhouse*
as he throws a pair of black stitches into the seam of a woman's flesh.
He has come from his third delivery this week, a boy, in a row house
where he thought he'd suffocate under a blanket of piety and prayer.
The sun's red flame in the window said something else was true,
and, washing up, he told a joke. The one about the Irish bartender
who asks whether his patron would like a second drink of whisky.
The saddle's cold, fangs of ice hang from the stirrups as he rides.

The horse knows a barn as a place out of the wind, wants to hurry.
Smiling, D.V. recalls the punchline: *No bird ever flew on one wing*
and lets the animal have its way. Passing a last house, he thinks
the hard gleam of the world softened, the blood-slosh and -froth
of terrible injury or difficult birth a memory the closed eye releases.
This time, it becomes a line of traincars slowing in the switching yard,
wheel-and-track braking noises at the decibel level of a muffled shout.
The rouged air is a mixture of coalsmoke and snow falling onto track
and traincar, and that awful need to believe in God or nothing at all.

## 4. The Mountain Physician's Apiary

consists of a dozen Langstroth hives in east-facing
placement, another dozen in south-facing placement,

all the hives on pallets. A boy sleeving the breeze
with smoke gathers honey from the shelves. Knows

escape board from queen excluder, propolis from comb.
And can calculate, at 16, bee space like the breast heft

of certain local women. The worker bees swim the air,
patterning ideograms for this thieving from the haves

to sweeten the coffee and sweet tea of the have-nots.
D.V. Bentley calls what he does a skill. *Doc* Bentley.

Who pays him as much as he'd earn in the mines.
And the youth moves about in the light and air.

Feels the feverish insects against his naked face,
the shake of bee-bodies as they calm like mystics

after revelation. He wouldn't name them that—
mystics—being blissfully ignorant of religion

beyond the living-fire, holy-roller antics he's
seen and fled. He doesn't hurry. He half-steps

with the respect of one who surveys the path
ahead for snakes, praying that his luck holds.

## 5. Boss

A husband to me said *servitude*. I was boss
of my little butter-and-egg delivery business.
Boss of a yellow '32 Ford with a rumble seat.
But my husband cuffed me. Took my money.
Smashed the Mason jar I used for a piggy bank.
And so I ran off. To parents. Home. To heal up.
I adored my room. The clean shrine of Childhood.
I couldn't stay there. My mother wouldn't hear of it.
But every time I went back to him, it was the same.
Soon, I'd be dodging the syncopated slaps and think,
*You've got to sleep sometime* then wouldn't do a thing.
Like abuse is the cost of buttering bread, raising kids.
There are ties that come unknotted. Doing my route,
if a man smiled at me, I'd smile back. Take my time.
Even if all the dogs of Neon barked in the road like
they were boss of that much of eastern Kentucky,
the scalloped hem of Nothing. I suppose I flew
the black flag of my own country in those days.
When they buried Quiller Bentley, my father,
in the Bentley-family cemetery at the Junction,
my brother D.V. put an arm around me. Walked
me down the hill to the homeplace, saying, *Sis,
we'll get you a divorce*. Like he was boss now.
He was running Neon by the time I ran the next
sonofabitch-bastard up a phone pole. Shot at him.
And they may have carted me off to a sanitarium,
but at least I didn't piss myself like Bob Beach—
married with kids of his own, fathering my child—
shaking his head and crying, seeming so far off.
Little pearls of teardrop coursing down his fat face
as he watched me squeeze a trigger that warmed
with some version of Hollywood-movie justice,
a heat like what I felt as I aimed and kept missing.

## 6. Adultery and Murder (for Some of Us) Smell Like Supper

which explains why the first time you see Lana Turner
in *The Postman Always Rings Twice* she's preceded
by a lipstick case rolling across a hamburger joint's
linoleum. She's blond, built like women used to be
when a few extra pounds at the hips said what it said
and the anticipatory sweetness of sex was drawn out
to a lot of alternating close-ups before the Big Fade.
John Garfield is tending a burger patty, his supper,

and the case rolls toward him at the speed of a slow
eye-blink. Since they're the only ones in the place,
he picks it up. Holds it out. But he doesn't move.
Not one sizzling, meat-on-the-grill inch toward her.
He's a guy answering a Man Wanted sign. Just that.
And whatever else has happened in his life thus far,
he's not about to be a sap for a woman. No matter
how breathtakingly well she may fill out the fabric

of a knotted-at-the-waist peasant blouse or define
what we pray is next but never is. She frosts him
with a smile, then takes the lipstick from his hand.
They both move at a glacial pace. I'll spare you talk
of angels and desire, any interlude in the slaughter.
Adultery and car-careening murder cancel contracts,
laws. Your soul's a cop's nightstick; their souls, too.
I'll just say: He let the hamburger blacken and burn.

No one—not even John Garfield—is up for what
comes after the wreck of the world as he's known it.
If you blame Lana Turner, you might as well blame
the wind for whipping around and shaping your hair
into a fin. Whatever he thought, seeing her he saw
something with the power to take away all hunger.
I guess you'd like to tell your children there are rules.
I suppose it helps to tell yourself something like that.

## 7. Sass

When I was thirty-two, I kicked the windshield out of a Ford Roadster while being dragged to an asylum in Lexington. What else could it be but sass? I wondered what they were doing, their hands all over me. Soon, though, it was clear: they thought me mad; and instead of being careful not to brush my breasts or hike my skirt and display undergarments and pale woman-skin, they weren't careful. No, they wrestled me as if I were an animal. I stopped kicking long enough to catch them off guard and broke off swearing at them, those men who meant me bodily harm. They meant to control me when they cried *Stop, Susan!* like knowing my name meant they knew all of my secrets. A man is vulnerable, too. The married one I ran up the phone pole, waving that forty-five, begged for his life as I fired. You can kick and gouge them in the groin, in the eyes. And they didn't suspect the strength of a mad woman to be equal to theirs. I wasn't going back without them wearing reminders that some women are a tale of sin and penance for sin; others are a whole other order of justice. If I screamed God's name, whose frail exposure was on display? Whose limbs wore scratch marks the color of a rooster's wattle? All I'd done was say *Fuck you* in a voice they'd remember to the grave. How fortunate they were, part of belief in a deity whose aim was to aid men. Because once you've worn the leather of restraints and felt the ah-ha jolt of electroshock, it's all the same day. Once you've borne the weight of bodies inside your body, bearing them outside is what it is, and harder. Let glass shatter and fall where it may. Let the faces of babes stare as if womankind were an empty sleeve to them. The ballast of a body isn't a thing to be carried lightly. They had the bottomland of my inheritance and the money from the egg business; they could have my curses, too. They were hellbent on breaking me when what I wanted was to whirl in a dancehall, young once, and say whatever came to mind, and loudly, since my life was my own, or was then; all that, a memory that flickers and gutters like a candle as if light were cruelty as much as anything.

## 8. Pine Mountain Overthrust Fault

D.V. Bentley learned that it runs through Letcher County,
the result of eons of pressures within the earth. The property
of rock strata to be acted upon by the movement of other rock.
How did D.V. know this? How can we be sure he knew this?
He owned a copy of *The Pattern of the Earth's Mobile Belts*
by Walter H. Bucher. Over breakfast once, D.V. told his wife,
my great-aunt Nettie, who then told her sister Frances Potter
in a moment of sisterly gossip: "Doctor reads an *awful* lot!"
Frances Potter, my maternal grandmother, then told me
as if an *a priori* love of revenant structures wants to flood

the eye with fresh ghosts. She said D.V. adored buildings.
Preferred limestone to brick. Brick to any sort of wood.
He built The Bank of Neon and then Bentley Drugstore.
Bentley Hotel. A theater called The Neon. An A & P.
It'd be more accurate to say: he paid to *have* them built.
D.V. had soft hands—a doctor's hands—which meant he
let others accomplish the drudgery of quarrying the stones.
For years, Stallard's Barber Shop was one of his tenants.
John Stallard cut his hair. Passed the time of day with him.
Maybe John listened to D.V. sing the praises of limestone—

hair falling to the scissors then the clippers humming softly,
low-humming as accompaniment to the words. Maybe he had
leukemia by then. Had begun trips to have his blood transfused.
If the hair collected in piles, it took the breeze and was scattered.
Maybe the doctor in him had accepted the last layer of Knowing
as the property of motion that thrusts a thing up, out of the way,
in favor of another. Whatever the case, he left a future hefted
by calloused, willing hands on a day like any other. Maybe
a crowd had gathered once to see what was taking shape,
rising from empty and emptier earth one stone at a time.

### 9.  The Spell for Summoning and Ending Rain

D.V. always put handcuffs on me before taking me back.
To the asylum in Lexington. But he didn't have Monroe,
his pal, along to help him. Which meant I might escape.
It was raining hard. He'd have to watch the road ahead.
When I got the cuffs up around his neck from behind,
across the back of the seat, it surprised him. He jerked.

I stopped being the Invisible Sister, quiet in back.
During the crash, which amazed even me in my state
of mad anger, I got a whack on the head. Blacked out.
We wound up in a coal-company hospital between Neon
and Hell for Certain. An attending doctor must've been kin
since he called D.V. "Uncle Doc." I woke to that voice.

A nurse with lipstick-red lips and red hair asked how I felt.
I felt like hell, my head hurt, so I said that—*I feel like hell.*
The whole thing was a lot like those spells my Welsh witch
granny tried to teach me as a girl: there are words for what
you want to have happen but they, the spells, those words,
mean more than you think. Say you need rain and cast

the spell for summoning rain. Then the valley floods.
Now you need to make it let up. No temple like a dry sky.
No love like having to wear handcuffs your doctor-brother
borrows when he needs to. No nudge to belief in the Unseen
like the sleight-of-hand of the cuffs around his neck, blood
dribbling onto bruised feminine hands like living sunlight.

## D. V. Bentley Day

Below the bald-eagle-rampant masthead for *The Mountain Eagle*,
the article says that he's sick. Stopped by Fleming Hospital recently
to receive a blood transfusion. It doesn't say he's dying of leukemia.
All those years of mounting his horse to ride for miles—in winter,
they freed ice-covered boots from the stirrups with his hand-axe.

Just a year before this commemoration, in nineteen fifty-four,
Elvis Presley had wandered into Sun Records to cut a second
acetate disc, which did nothing. Elvis drove a delivery truck.
Folks forced to pick up and live anywhere other than home
are like someone with a failing lung shouting at the world.

Maybe shouts are all they have. Maybe the shouts can turn
to singing. And maybe that singing gets played on the radio.
My parents had left Kentucky for a two-bedroom brick house.
A kid, I was carted to the tribute after the long drive from Ohio.
After my dad finished shift-work at Frigidaire in Moraine City.

I'm told D.V. held me and asked my name. Smiled at *Roy Glenn*.
My mother says the train on the Clinchfield line, departing Neon,
as a sign of respect, refrained from blowing its whistle that day.
I like to summon the train cars. Wheels, track, railbed singing
and Doc Bentley waving from his open Cadillac convertible.

# A Partial Accounting of the Lost Years of Susan Bentley Accompanied by the Lefty Frizell Song "If You've Got Money, Honey"

We'd see my grandmother Bentley on her furloughs
from Eastern State Hospital if she was allowed to call
to be picked up in Lexington. She'd been committed
from the time she chased a man up a telephone pole,
emptying an heirloom .45 Colt in his general direction
at the Junction in Neon, and her brother D. V. Bentley
had arranged for her not to be jailed. When we'd drive
south from Dayton across the Ohio River into Kentucky,
my father would always ask my mother to instruct me
as to what would be all right to ask my grandmother
and what might add fuel and ignite her famous rage.
If we pulled over for lunch at the Frisch's Big Boy
on the Cincinnati side of the Ohio, I'd get to order
by pressing the button on a call box above the silver
swivel tray and answering the anonymous Someone.
My father played the Cadillac's radio all the way there
and back, leaving it off the few hours my grandmother
was in the car. Why? It had been left on once, the radio,
because who knew, and a Lefty Frizell song set her off.
She swore piercingly, saying, "What's *that* horseshit?"
Started in pounding my father's neck and shoulders
from the back seat. When money ran out for her care,
the Department of Mental Health Eastern State Hospital
sent a letter signed *Very truly yours, Logan Gragg, M.D.*
It began *Dear Sir*, was on embossed letterhead stationary
stamped with the seal of the Commonwealth of Kentucky.
It said she was ready to be picked up. Like all those years
hadn't happened or were the stuff of memory, unworthy
of any elaboration in a letter that was signed and dated.
No mention of reasons Bob Beach had fled for his life.
No paragraph as to D. V. having to sell the homeplace
to keep a sister out of jail or prison and in a sanitarium.
Nothing of the nostalgia she might feel for a girlhood
before she learned to shoot and was given the pistol.

## Fountain Filled with Blood

As a kid, songs they sang made you want to run.
Myrtle Dellinger and Blanche Barnett and Granny,
the twang of their raw voices contending with ideas
of union in a cauldron of mining folk past singing.
Maybe someone had died young or from violence.
Maybe they were getting together at Christmastime.
My granny would start, steering by instinct. Joined
by Myrtle and Blanche, her daughters, my aunts,
rocking as if the life-force was entering or leaving
the body, traveling in and out on vectors of Spirit.
Those three could fill all the rooms of a row house.
They'd drown out *Ed Sullivan*, if it had been left on.
Over any sort of noise, they sang *a cappella*—Italian
for "in the manner of the church"—or unaccompanied.
Words spilled, a syrup—*there is a fountain filled
with blood / the blood of our brave mining men*—
as voices loosed a desperate ecstasy. Longing.
Of course sometimes they made up the lyrics.
Like one line Granny repeated: *And the blood
came trickling down* . . . Something improvised
because the world is faithless and thieving
and beautiful in the same breathless instant.
Fluent in the songs of cars, dashboard lights,
churches too impoverished to afford hymnals,
they kept it up; one or the other woman nodding
to signal a solo like they were at the Ryman,
onstage at the Grand Ole Opry. The poor—
which is what we were—know how to sing.

## Winter Elegy

She wants us to stop sledding. And to come in.
At the foot of the hill behind our house, she raises

a hand to the side of her mouth. Shouts *Bobby!* then
*Jimmy!*—then louder: *Rascals!* We are her grandkids

and stir the way memories do: at their own speed.
Bobby is Huckleberry Finn and so wants not to

hear or answer. And then there's Jimmy—Jim.
Jim is Bob's apostle-shadow. His little brother.

First to come back to the house, I'm beside her,
our granny, in the carport. Sloughing off my boots.

Bob and Jim keep it up. Together, they seem to be
like branches the wind has heaped with snowfalls,

their smallish shoulders avalanching at every step.
Now she calls out again, sees it's useless, and so

is pausing to re-button the coat she has thrown on—
the coat is gray, its buttons as big as a fat-kid's fist.

She commences crossing drifts in her house shoes.
Threatens to climb the hill to the top. Not wanting

to swear, she tries: *Lord Jesus, give me strength!*
Once and again in her Appalachian uber-twang.

Her voice finds a kind of diminuendo as down
they come—into the snow-tenanted afternoon,

the runners of sleds dragging on rocks, making
scrapings that are neither hymn nor absolution.

## Staggering

A taxi idles. The driver comes around. A door is opened.
My grandfather Beach staggers and is dragged, struggling,
to be handed a twenty-dollar bill and deposited into the taxi.
My father: *I told him not to show his face around me again.*

I overhear these details as a child. The never-repeated story
he told my mother, my young father who called in ordnance
in Korea, artillery shells that rained down bright black death
from great distances, who recreated the night a soused father

came to where he was staying in Kentucky after his discharge;
Bob Beach, his biological father, a blood relative by chance,
an old man who came to see his son, staggering up the steps
to a rented house to ask—no, *beg*—forgiveness far too late.

In the book of our family stories, this one was like a storm
where the stars disappear and then are everywhere at once,
all the features in silhouette and drawn in part, an obituary
implied like a flash of light on a hill in a foreign country.

I could hear the house he rented back then exhale grief
as he turned his life inside out like a shirt from a dryer
or off a clothesline, sleeves wrong and out of alignment.
He had nothing decent to say about that night, my father,

or the wretched man who misstepped and was carried.
He recalled rain had moved in but without the requisite
thunder we use to decipher distance, counting seconds
as we watch silhouetted windows mirror and go dark.

## Kentucky Love Story

*One need not weep romantic tears for them,*
*But when the last moonshiner buys his radio,*
*And the last, lost wild-rabbit of a girl*
*Is civilized with a mail-order dress,*
*Something will pass that was American,*
*And all the movies will not bring it back.*

—Stephen Vincent Benet, "John Brown's Body"

*for Stevie Conley*

When she is nude, barring a stretch mark or two
and her tendency to eschew black gartered stockings,
his lust for his wife Blanche is like a swallow of moonshine—
impossible to down without loving the reviving nature of it.
These days, any thoughts of her with that Belcher boy, Johnny,
can push him over the edge. The rumors are a taunt. Nothing
that Blanche will admit to. Except to say, Never happened.
He was away in the South Pacific. Serving in the Seabees.
Rumors are why Bill Barnett and Blanche's brother Bill Potter
are lying on their bellies with TNT pilfered from stockpiles
of some eastern Kentucky coalfield. Like more than a few
who stayed behind during the war, Johnny has it coming.
And Bill sees his duty as making sure that Johnny gets his.
With four kids, Bill Barnett volunteered for the Army. Blanche,
newly shorn of all hope of a helpmate, was left to fend for herself.
It's a story of a woman sleeping with a man after a dance and whose
child is whose become very much in doubt. So there are two Bills
on a hillside and Johnny Belcher needing blown to smithereens.
Between pulls on a fifth of bourbon whiskey, J.T.S. Brown,
Bill says, "I'll duck-walk my dumb ass down this-here slope.
I'll light this and toss it. And run like hell. You wait here."
He pats the TNT in a pocket of his long black coat. Smiles.
The other Bill seems about to open his mouth and complain.
He doesn't. He points to the silhouette of Johnny's oldest

waltzing onto the porch. Which means that no one named
Belcher will be killed or die tonight in an eerie hollow
in a region named from a mispronunciation of a Cherokee
word for *the land that lies south of the Ohio River.* It seems
mistakes are as good as it gets if you're waiting for the world
to answer for lies it tells you about itself on the way to truth.

## The Velocity of a Bullet Is Absolute

### 1

Before my cousin mentioned the puppies, I hadn't thought
a mother would kill her young, and even after he mentioned it,

the deaths, I preferred to consider his dog to be one of a kind,
an anomaly. How else to account for torn up pup bodies?

It seemed natural, at 10, to blurt out, *I'd shoot her.*
A boy has nothing to do with contingencies. To him,

an *in media res* world is serial, undiscovered absolutes.
The solipsism of childhood is well-known. A child grows,

and before he or she does we expect less. Or stop all of that
by offering a loaded .22 pistol, saying, Go ahead. Take charge.

In this, he was like the fathers brothers uncles—mothers—
who walk us to deep water and toss us in, saying, Swim.

I hated him. Hated the heft and weight of the revolver.
Hated the State of Virginia and everyone named Billy.

I hated being told to squeeze, not jerk, the trigger.
He squatted in summer earth by his exhausted dog,

separating her away from the remainder of the litter.
She went, answering some fresh memory of kindness.

He motioned where I should put the round (or rounds).
Stepped back and a little away from the panting dog,

acting as if he had considered and believed I'd shoot.
I can say now, after 50 years, why I hated him then.

Because he took the gun. Before I could act. Raised
the blue-black barrel. Fired. Bent down. Fired again.

**2**

They lied he didn't use a Christmas-gift Remington 12-gauge pump
and kept the casket closed. Both parents were the picture of grief—

both Bill and Blanche had to be sedated, both had to be kept away
from Banks & Craft Funeral Home where they took him. Neon

wasn't dead in those days. You could sit down to a cheeseburger
and fries and a "Co-cola" at Tucker's Drugstore & Soda Fountain.

You could rent a room at the Bentley Hotel, where Hazel Bentley
would fill you in on news and gossip from as far away as Frankfort.

There was D.V. Bentley's brick Colonial mansion on Main Street
on the end of town by the A & P, the house Hazel lived in with her

crazy sister, Betty Ellen. You could buy a ticket to the Neon Theater
and watch Dennis Hopper and Peter Fonda murdered in *Easy Rider*.

You could haggle for a good price on a Mercury at Harlow Motors.
Top off the tank at Howard Collier's Pure Oil. Banks & Craft was

still burying citizens of that much of eastern Kentucky, carting off
the wages of black lung in a Cadillac hearse with hand-painted logo.

Staggeringly drunk miners vanished from Saturday-night streets,
the War on Poverty had come and gone. To this Neon, we brought

Billy Barnett. A dying small town. Some paved streets drenched
in blood-letting and so could receive a body with a stalk of head

and almost no face. He went into the ground in Whitesburg—
on a day when what a man is or isn't offers little impediment

to diggers on furlough from the mines, their dissatisfied wives,
men who'll finish work under a sky too immense for memory.

## Members of the Primitive Baptist Church Attend a Creek Baptism by Submersion

The line of worshipers collects by an August creek bank.
Their song goes *Shall we gather at the river, the beautiful*
*the beautiful river...* The creek isn't much during summer,
though it will all but cover a convert to his or her waist.
A woman in white is holding a man's fedora. Another
is wading out from the bank into russet-colored water.
Frances Collier Potter is here, hair bobby-pinned up.

In epistolary First Corinthians the Apostle Paul says
that the hair of any woman is her glory and covering.
Her pastor says it says that. Adds salvation is no joke.
If it is a joke, grace, the punchline is accepting Christ
with the faith of a child: meaning as blindly trusting
as anyone, male or female, gets in Letcher County.

Ask anyone about Letcher County and you'll hear
that if God plays favorites, this isn't one of those.
Ask about the Redeemer any time but don't ask
Frances Collier Potter about a child she lowered
into black as familiar as the slap from a brother
or husband. In the fish-slaughtering coal mine
run-off, closer to an understanding of laurels

than the supernatural, she lets go the memory
of star thistles of frost on glass after the death.
Even if it's true that good moonshine covers
a multitude of sins, this is the wrong woman
to fuck with. Glory or no glory, she hikes up
her cotton robes and goes in to put one eye
to the task of keyholing the door to mercy.

## Eggs and Butter and Milk and Cheese

This morning, a starless Kentucky either side of the road,
she drives her Ford Roadster, dispensing eggs and butter

and milk and cheese. Citizens of the Junction are stirring,
quick-dressing to the racket of blackbirds, going to doors.

If they aren't white or kin or lucky enough to have a tab,
they rifle pants pockets or Mason jars for required coins.

This is someone familiar with handling quart bottles and
cartonless eggs, wheels of cheese sectioned and wrapped

in the manner that mountainfolk have said yes to for years.
Accept that butter is white and sliced in blocks of a weight

reckoned at a fair market value of one buffalo-head nickel.
Figure this to be the liberation other women only dream of.

Not long after firstlight, she'll have delivered what she has,
emptying her rumble seat to a town of ossified row houses

where a radio, if there is one, is tuned to a country station.
She's no fool. Assume the .45 under the driver's-side seat

and the Bentley disposition and untenanted heart to use it.
Concede the world will thieve everything she earns. More.

## Train for Glory

After the Washing of the Feet, an old woman gets up.
She reaches into a basket. Takes out a couple of snakes.
The sound of rattlesnakes? Pennies nickels dimes poured
from a Mason jar, if loose change was as unpredictable as
an Old Testament God or a job in a mine where generations
exhaust hope. She drapes a snake over each palm and thumb,
welcomes a show of fangs. The pleats of her skirt are starched
and each reptile, in turn, starts to rub against the crenellations.
Pleats may spark trust. But then the gospel of one-note hissing
isn't music; though neither is the slamming of the screen door,
the loud exit of an unbeliever from Hemphill. Lose the snakes,
the congregant is my grandmother's sister or might as well be.
Her hair is pulled up in a too-tight bun—now she motions me
onstage. I get up and go outside. In waist-high grasses tonight
in the hills are nations of snakes. Especially in mid-August.
But I should be halfway to Fleming-Neon before anything
venomous stirs in the wet dark washing my feet as I run.

.

Granny said it needed to arrive without delay, her train for glory.
I'm sure I know what she meant now. And I had some idea then.
At 7, though, I hadn't ridden a train yet. Let alone one to Glory.
She watched Billy Graham Crusades. And made me watch, too.
Glory sounded like it was a town in her east-Kentucky girlhood.
Maybe it showed up, out of nowhere, like the preacher on TV.
I didn't know how she existed, forever crying and raising her
hands toward the ceiling or longed-for Heaven. Calling out.
The way she did it, her brand of worship, if it had been washing
on a galvanized washboard then she would have rawed her hands.
I didn't imagine this applied to my life. I hadn't earned damnation.
I brought her the last unopened can of peaches from the kitchen—
Glory Foods produced peaches and I thought it would be funny.
I handed her those and she went back through what she'd said
about Glory. She got the joke—because she waved the can.
Said the opener and spoon would be the last word on that.

## Near Hell for Certain, Kentucky

That summer, I lost a prized bear there.
The Teddy bear granny Potter bought me
in the bus station in Ohio. Jenkins, Kentucky
was the endpoint of the Greyhound line in 1962,
but my granny ensnared some off-duty taxi driver
by promising him ten dollars if he would "carry us"—
an eight-year-old boy with a Teddy bear, her, and
her slate-gray Samsonite suitcase—from Jenkins,
out of a blistering July-noon in eastern Kentucky,
to Hell for Certain. Which was in Leslie County.
Turns out, America Webb lived there. Her sister.
America had a deep well with good, cold water.
A widow with no kids. Raised tea roses in the
postage-stamp yard of her white row house.
America *adored* my granny. And my granny
adored America right back. But I'm digressing—
I must have left my bear there, near Hell for Certain:
I don't recall having it in my eight-year-old arms after
waving goodbye to America through the back window
of a cab. I'm 99% sure that's what must have happened.
However, it could have been something else altogether.
The bear left in some drugstore café on the return trip,
Kentucky to Ohio, its fake-glass eyes reversing **Dayton**.
Regardless, I was told that Teddy bear would be my last.
And I was asked, *Can't you hold on to anything?* Until she
died—Mazie Frances Collier Potter, my mother's mother—
I didn't know that a death can make you feel what I felt:
like you'd never leave off looking for that loved thing.

*Body of a Deer by a Creek in Summer*

*for Matt*

The shadows of sycamores are delible with a weight
of days of rain, the runoff roofed with blue butterflies
and splish-splashes locals decrypt as leaf-boat traffic.

Ants fashion an elegy to hotels from a deer carcass.
Whatever is meant by an animal afterlife, this is that.
If tracks are those of a perfect walker, the hind hoof

falling almost exactly in the print of the front hoof,
the track and straddle pattern roughly a straight line—
some flesh doesn't so much love travel as live by it

before falling. Maybe the deer saw the white flash
as a car clipped it where it stood. Where the road
extends for miles through a gloom of shade trees,

past credible rope bridges to hillside row houses.
We know it made it here, the deluge inundating
bushes where it felt its heart beat with starlight

and stubborn exertion rimmed with last breath,
contiguous waters low-hissing like a neon sign.
Maybe any August is a hymn meant to be sung

in the open by a creek with thunder choiring and
lightning strikes and a fire-and-brimstone sermon
on the death we carry with us and wear like a skin.

## Walking Hills

Just over a rise, I glimpse a starred truck windshield,
a beveled dresser-mirror, the reverse lives of the trees.
I'm walking the switchbacks from the ridge and down,
skidding, grabbing at a sassafras branch here and there.
A friend has been sending emails about haunted places
in Parkersburg. I think Ghosts and stare into the mirror
become a slope to a river, the river, the flanking hills.
In this light, apparitions are legion. Flashes of anger
and escape from home, if home is these hollows.

Some days, I could bet myself a fifth of scotch
this much of the earth is God's country and win,
but today a busted windshield is splendoring into
the unbroken part of itself. I'm rectangular, a casket
with eyes and hair and a mouth—wasn't it Mark Twain
who said humans make graveyards of the beautiful places?
It starts to rain. I duck inside the ruined truck. The roof
is like correspondence with a friend: not much cover.
Rain becomes the calm and storms and calm again

that is Appalachia: isolating voices, old-old hurts,
and a need to hurt others some carry like a handsel.
I'm told that I'm a threatening presence. Dangerous.
And I've been told to lower my voice when speaking
so that bystanders won't think that I'm about to strike.
But I am about to strike: I begin to bust the windshield
the rest of the way out as I would've done years ago
surrounded by big-hearted boys from around here.
Boys who became men who make others nervous.

## River Baptism

Some were on the trampled bank in their Sunday best.
Some were boys hiding above in the trees and the rest were
in the water. We had slithered through that summer-Kentucky
undergrowth so we wouldn't miss out. And had climbed an oak.
We'd overheard granny Potter say the locals would be acting out
circus-come-to-town Pentecostalism, baptizing (by immersion)
in the mine-runoff-polluted North Fork of the Kentucky River.
Converts dropped the Hefty-bagged change of clothes carted
across God rendering fields and thickets. My cousins Roger
and Ricky Dellinger were in the tree, too. They pronounced
the last name like the gangster John Herbert Dillinger who
broke out of jail in Ohio in 1933 and skedaddled that way:
toward the Letcher County Line and some outlaw-family
who were to be his salvation. Roger worshipped Dillinger.
Habitually, that summer, he pilfered apples pears peaches
in the IGA while his mother Myrtle shopped. He'd toss
the core, the pay-as-you-go rule not in force for Roger.
Ricky Dellinger wanted to preach since his mother said
there was a hell and she wanted to miss it. All their lives,
and mine, she had read aloud—mostly to Ricky and me—
from the Bible, immersing us in a demon-snake theodicy,
Adam and Eve and an aboriginal Eden. That day, though,
a mountain woman was praising the open boat of the air
and coming up from the russet water in such an ecstatic
way that even Roger listened and tried not to spoil it—
spoil us catching sight of a pure omnibenevolent God.
Sometimes a whole country can be as rotten as Roger.
Sometimes a limb creaks and a congregation looks up.
Sometimes you almost fall and someone catches you
and you're not sure who it was. That day, however,
America wore a white dress that was mortared to her
seemingly incorruptible skin. And she was forgiven.

## Show Me the Face of My Great-Grandfather Before He Burned

Take back the afternoon light at Neon Junction in Letcher County,
the crying of my father in infancy on the porch in a basket of sheets.
Take back the stories of Quiller Bentley, my great-grandfather, setting
ablaze the underbrush growing over his field rather than labor to clear it.
Take back rogue gusts turning flames in his direction and then the flames
encircling him in retreat. Take back a narcotic blur of screams and a body
in rebellion throughout one night and a day and then another night. Leave
me his bland face before all this and I will give you back the ruby skin of
lesser burned places, his failing to account for an insurgency in the wind.

We are, after all, the sum of our mistakes as well as answering for them.
I forfeit wanting an answer for swindles after palm-to-palm handshakes,
the whole of the history of the first Kentuckians and the theft-by-contact
and ages of poverty at the hands of armies of robber barons. I'll forego
remembrance of joy at seeing my grandmother Bentley's face brighten
at any suggestion of leaving Neon Junction—not the thing but an echo
of the thing, not sorrow or crying out after sorrow but one man raising
himself to curse God and fall back onto cool sheets turned and turning
midnight black and pomegranate red, the colors of his difficult dying.

161

## Coal Town Saturday Night

*Bow and swing your partner to the left
bow and swing your partner to the right,
listen to the music and hold your lady tight,
it's a coal town Saturday night . . .*

—Randall Hylton, "Coal Town Saturday Night"

We read the heartbreak stories in *The Mountain Eagle*,
hear we're violent people—a seeping wound is adjacent

to the stubby beginnings of what appear as angel-wings.
Which is to say, truth coexists with what's exceptional.

Here's a truth: Junior Tucker shot my uncle Ed Potter
and Johnny Belcher gunned down my uncle Earl. Both

uncles were murdered because the men who fought them
feared a colossal beating. They testified to that. A judge

ruled, in each case, the killing was an act of self-defense.
The difference between manslaughter and self-defense,

between a just judge and one fighting his own fear—
is the difference between having to fight to live, living

without a reason, and simply hating that you were born.
It may be the case that you believe in angels, devils, a God.

Maybe a God who looks down on the ghosts some men are
in Letcher County, Kentucky. The lit coal of their anger.

## Angry Men

### 1. Without a Wish or a Word to Slow the Falling

—Ralph Black, "The Theory and Practice of Angels,"
*The Southern Review*, Autumn 2008

What I was doing watching *Peter Pan* while my father
and a woman went into a bedroom-Neverland I don't know.
I don't know why his adultery didn't register, even at 7,
any more than that Mary Martin was a woman. I was there,
at the rear of the woman's house, hearing the clock-tick
inside the crocodile of Conscience, waiting for this much
of the night to be over and to go into the kitchen, her kitchen,
and play penny-ante poker. I was in front of the television
for a good two hours waiting, and I know there is a quiet
in the house of a stranger and a look you get when that
stranger comes out of her bedroom, having made love
to your father. The lover he took that year wanted me
to win at poker. Her hand touched mine when my stack
of coins was gone. And I think Peter Pan may have gifted
the children with that look—a word of encouragement—
to make believers of them after the first of many falls
before they flew. The awful truth is that such falling is
the end of believing for most of us. He didn't look at me
when he came out of the woman's bedroom, at the table
playing poker or sometime later in the car, driving home,
the ante of my complicity to remind me whose son I was.
And he didn't ask me whether, or if, I'd liked *Peter Pan*.
Didn't tell me what this was about or what to say, later,
if my mother asked where we'd gone. What we'd done.
I don't know what makes a man betray a woman, but
I do know you're not a kid forever since no Tinkerbell
materialized anywhere near Dayton, Ohio that night.
He drove and the headlights of oncoming cars conjured
nothing approaching fairies. I knew there weren't fairies.
Maybe a pirate or two sailing to riches or flying to ruin.

## 2. Mantle Dying

*for Theresa Ann Aleshire Williams*

If I needed a hero, you'd be that guy—
a second liver in the busted gut, the sudden

knowledge of mortality that has you fielding
questions about the cancer and what comes next.

Everyone's going where you are, yet they marvel.
Maybe DiMaggio was right to marry the movie star.

For sure, characterizing your fairy-tale life as wasted
is tacky. But then you flash that Commerce-Oklahoma-

aw-shucks grin and lean into the bank of microphones.
Who knew you'd teach us about dying and not wanting

death to appear in the way 1956 had: out of nowhere.
Who knew you had to be the Christ and swing a bat.

We aren't all champions, but you've got us hoping
we rise from our hospital sick beds as if the light

is wrong or has reminded us we were holding on
for someone else. At the end, we want to believe

you were daydreaming about the leggy models
draped over you in the Brylcreem commercials.

### 3. *Upon Being Called a Hillbilly in Iowa*

John Steinbeck understood angry men, called them interesting,
and I'm one. A man and angry. And now this man I work with,
who says he's been everywhere playing lead and rhythm guitar
in a rock 'n roll band, has called me a hillbilly. Sure, he says it
with a smile the size of Dubuque like it's just something to say
when men are getting to know one another. And so there it is,
that tingling sensation at the back of the neck. It doesn't matter
anymore how much or little my heart is written on by cruelty.
It doesn't matter that I should have learned something by now
about the way men whittle at one another like a block of wood.
To fashion something ugly to replace something else, who knows.
Today, as usual, the fellow knows better but doesn't apologize,
except by continuing to talk like the real problem is with me.
Time again for patching the wound with whatever's at hand.
With words or a blow to the face. Maybe both. Maybe neither.
Time to choke down a sense that no man is part of all he meets
till he meets it. Or doesn't because his daughter is in the room
and too interested in what he may or may not be about to do.

### 4. Sid Hatfield, the Sheriff of Matewan, West Virginia, Has His Say

I'm not one to brag, but how many dead do you know who raise themselves up from 15 bullet wounds on some courthouse steps? Does it offend you the last was to the brain and I'm still holding forth, speaking truth to power? Some of the rest of the departed should be so lucky as to resurrect in a poem, touching the living again with words that resonate—I know, it's not a word we used a lot in those days in West Virginia but it's a word the dead know—because whatever good we do does that: echoes like one long stutter. I stood in the street that day and emptied both my Colt revolvers into a throng of coal-company thugs, killing at least two of the "sonsabitches"—there's a word for you, one that rises in anger like men will, some women too, if you push them. I don't mourn the men I sent to Perdition or the way they died in the railbeds, skull and brain matter mixing into a sluice of breath and blood and coal dust because of what some do for money. Why not offer a worker a fair wage? A worker, man or woman, can wait longer than grass springing up under trees hardened to human suffering. Why not watch smiles spreading on faces of generations of children who know only going to bed with full bellies? Why not let them believe the very best about us before they die? There is no end to bullets, with trajectories of sorrow and discontent and mayhem. And I don't want back the ones I loosed. And they, the sonsabitches who shot me, wouldn't want back those they poured into me that last day I could feel anything. But I would like to take the hand of a child and lead it away from the gore and then into the garden that even Matewan is. Look how blood vanishes, how the rain had the final word on what constitutes a union and ran on despite its precious freight. The rain *is* blood, more or less. It glows with violent change whatever we say.

## 5. 1946

Ed has come home to Neon from Ashland Pen
to the north, having served a year and two months
for the wounding of a US Army major in India.
He's pissed, sure, but who isn't in these hills?
A bad discharge doesn't mean disgrace, either.
Most of the male population of Letcher County
has been in some sort of scrape with the Law.
Hillfolk are dangerous when shoved or shot at.
Ed Potter wants not to be told he looks a lot like
John Garfield since what he hears is *Pretty Boy*.
One more idle hour and he may explode yet again.
Neon looks different as he walks from the Junction—
the way the interior walls of a B-17 Flying Fortress
will look different in different light, then familiar
as you stand in the door about to jump, then jump
shouting the Americanized name of that Apache
who bested the Army long enough to get famous.
When was the Bentley place bricked bright red?
Just when did D.V. Bentley get so prosperous?
Ed is ready to profit from his stretch in the pen,
prepared to holler *Geronimo!* and jump into life
after war and ransacking an overseas world for
the purpose of getting even. Ol' Doc Bentley
may need him to cut brush from bottomland
or swing a pick. Polish his convertible. Now,
as he passes the house, he sees lights burning
with a radiance that says they're not gas lamps.
When did Neon get electric like Ashland Pen?
He needs someone to answer a few questions.
The Commonwealth of the State of Kentucky
owes him a clarification. And a decent meal
like one he had sat down to when that major
staggered into him. Spilling whiskey. Acting,
back on his feet, as if nothing had happened.

## 6. Vengeance

It's a long time now since Junior Tucker
shot my uncle Ed and then choked to death
on a toothpick from the A&P grocery store.
Ironically, a man whose initials were A and P
had come to my grieving grandmother to ask
if she wanted Junior Tucker dead. Murdered.
She told me that A.P. asked her to say the word
and he'd shoot Junior. Stab him, if she needed
to know that he'd died slowly. My grandmother
said she told A.P. she prayed, for days, and been
shown a verse: *Vengeance is mine, sayeth the Lord,
and I will repay.* I'm paraphrasing, it's been years.
Maybe you've lost someone like that, someone
unrecognized for their gifts. For the great gift of
their presence. To make her grandchildren aware
of the world in which they lived, its seamless dark
and an occasional ray of light in a room, she read
from a book devoted to the notion of vengeance,
the King James Version of The Bible. She read it
to a boy whose name she sang to a failed orchard
when it was dinnertime. When she called, I'd hear
the cries from a branch inaccessible to most adults,
given their weight and inability to climb. If she was
mistaken, letting a murderer live a year or two longer,
praying to be shown how to keep the windows of
the heart open to the likelihood of a caring God
and some form of forgiveness, who am I to say?
It took a while, and a toothpick, but he did die.

## 7. Obituary

*"I doubted my composure—
my ability to compose—"*

Peter Schmitt, "My Father's Obituary," *Renewing the Vows*

He was watching PBS, *The Civil War*, fed up
with channels with commercials and Charlie Sheen,
and because, it turns out, the terminally ill—
some, at least—have a hard-on for battlefields.
He wasn't dead yet, my pops, the rot of lung
and prostate cancers hadn't finished him,
but it would, and soon. So he sat me
down beside him. Said I should write something
they could put in the newspaper afterwards.
A way to calibrate the timepiece he used
to keep track of his life. A calendar with marginalia
and appointments indelibly inked in. This man
who bruised nearly everyone around him
wanted me, the Writer, his son, to sum up
seventy-eight years of love and war
and the rest, his way of being alive, existence
according to one born in 1932, et cetera.
I begged off, saying I'd tried before,
in poems, and *that* hadn't been to his liking.
I wish I could remember why they call those pockets
of silence near a battlefield "acoustic shadows"—
we were talking, and I caught only fragments,
a small part, nothing that would serve understanding:
much like eulogizing anyone's life. I wish I could
be sure it had something to do with how sound travels,
how observers can see what is taking place
and yet are swaddled in a mysterious lapse of noise.
I wish I could say how they decided
that some form of explanation was more important
than the simple comfort and blessing it is
not to be among those undertaking the dying,
to be that far removed from the fighting.

## 8. Roy "Judge" Bean Goes Hillbilly on a Defendant

*If I'm not a Kentuckian anymore,* thought the Judge—
and thoughts of the Big Sandy River in spring rose in him,
*maybe I'm all the law there is in this part of west Perdition,*
*maybe there's a dollar or two in this*—but his hill-born brain
made him remember these were not his people and whatever
cruelty he exacted upon them was, well, money in the bank.
He had had a rope around his neck. Been dragged through
the chaparral. Lost one testicle to a thorn bush, thank you;
saying hello anywhere in Texas like slapping a rattlesnake.
The usual human foolery bored him more than a fair fight.
And so, most mornings, he started by rendering a verdict
on an Unfortunate with his hands and feet tied, pockets
already rifled through, a look in his eyes surrendering
thoughts of fairness, waiting to hear *Guilty!* shouted
in service of the truth about west Texas. Absolutely
the sort of thing a stranger should keep to himself
for fear of winding up like this, about to be hanged
in the only manner possible in such treeless country,
an order shouted, in Spanish, to a horse who knows
or has a pretty good idea about what is happening
for the unpardonable sin of disparaging the thorns
then the whole bush the Judge had grown fond of,
having been left a cherished-and-residual "left nut"
which he dedicated, thereafter, to the quest of being
found worthy to meet the Jersey Lily, Lily Langtry.
Never to be a Kentuckian again and happy, married
to the awful fact of what any man will and must do
to survive, he secures the knotted rope to the neck.
Says a word, in English, meaning *Fucked again.*
Then smiles. Booms out a high, cackling laugh
filled with the light of forested spaces and hawks
falling from the sky through clean, righteous air.

## 9. *Early Spring in Ohio*

*for Stevie Conley*

In the beginning, her stories were beautiful.
Mostly about girlhood and barn dances. Boys.
Then my grandmother let it slip she'd lost sons.
Early spring in Ohio, and she walked outside
without finishing her sentence. I went, too.
Our development lawn wasn't green yet,
and the sky looked like it was deciding
if there was a blue the world might wear
or at least try on. I had heard I had uncles

who'd been murdered. Heard it whispered
like that a bush wouldn't blossom because
our neighbors were Mexican, the mother
a *curandero.* Which my grandmother said
meant that she was little better than a witch.
That year, Comanche Drive was one big epic
of upheaval and going on, my father "traveling"
and Mother working. It is a matter of no great
importance to me now whether the neighbors

were Mexican, the mother a caster of spells,
or another nationality—say, Greek or Cuban—
but I want to remember why my grandmother
stopped talking that day, and why her retelling
of the deaths had me following barefoot. *At least
you're safe here*, she told me. Absurd thing to say,
surely, to a boy of 5 to whom Ohio had so far been
a home, and that home pretty much unthreatened.
She looked down at my lack of shoes and socks,

and reconsidered the story, where she'd left off
and how it had ended up tossing us both outside
into the world of the *curandero* who might have

had the cure for her grieving, for all she knew.
She didn't say she was sorry, only *Let's get*
*you inside*—while the young maples furred
with that first green-and-greener-still and
she wiped her eyes with a petticoat hem
and I turned so as not to see too much.

## The Rape of Edith Rose

He shares this story, my father, the night before he dies.
After the morphine, he tells me he and his sister Edith slept

together. She was 13. Had breasts. And shuddered, he said,
as the uncle came into the bedroom to force himself on her.

As a result, he says, Edith Rose is the way she is. Meaning
a little crazy, a drunk by anyone's standards. Their mother

had landed in a sanitarium, an insubordinate female defiant
in the face of victimization. After, her kids were farmed out

to an aunt named Minerva and a man who gave no warning
what he was capable of. Sometimes twice in the same night.

Tonight, he's speaking as if this happened to both of them.
Which it did, if you consider having had to pretend sleep

while your sibling is taken like that. He told me it, they,
the violations, went on for years. That they only stopped

when she married. He rattled off how Minerva was the
Roman goddess of poetry who leapt from the split-open

head of Jupiter. He smiled an exhausted, halved smile.
Fell back against the dark vein of a bedsheet shadow—

what does it mean to say we carry stories to the point
of death? Just that mercy has a beginning and an end.

## Appalachian Zombies

An impromptu militia assembles without being summoned.
There. See them move as if their vertebrae were on a swivel.
If existence is proof of anything, it's that life is an autopsy

in progress. One palms a lit Marlboro against bluish skin,
though without the stings of dissimilarity and clan identity
that sign a self like those other burn-scars of dubious origin.

Note the shuffle. If dreams were Mason jars of moonshine
and wishes were meth, any dark hollow in Coal Country
would have filled with happier hearts by now. As it is,

even songbirds here commit suicide, voluntarily flying
into the glass storefront of the CVS. To break their necks.
An integrated platoon of the undead pauses by a rent-a-sign

that asserts *Only the Believers in Jesus Christ Will Survive.*
We could use more panic where the ruined future is concerned.
If this is slapstick, this feeding on one another as at a picnic

where Jack Hale brings hot dogs and June Tolliver the buns,
why isn't it funny? Now the ghouls overtake a father and son.
In the chemical light by a parking lot, the boy is scooped up

and rescued. Foot-draggers sconce the car door. One leaves
red flowerets of signature bite marks on the man's forearm.
Even this insensible, they taste the coal dust in the blood.

## The Leatherwood Ghost Story

My father and Edith, his sister, went to visit their mother
in a private sanitarium in Frankfort where she was committed.
My father was back from Korea, Edith was between husbands.
They were on their way home, driving and talking. No moon.
It was his car, my father's, bought with the last of the money
saved during his three years in the army. He was at the wheel.
Says he looked away for a second. Took his eyes off the road
and ran into a creek. The creek bed was bone-dry but he hit
something. Busted both front tires. They were stuck. Nothing
for miles. Not a car or a truck or a human being as they rolled
down the windows and heard the hum of the eternal present.
They piled out. Started walking up the hollow toward a light
he figured was a house with electricity, rural electrification
rare but not unheard of in the hills in 1953. They walked—
remember: no 9-1-1 or cellphones—at road's edge in the dark.
My father said he felt a *tap-tap* on the shoulder. Said he told
Edith, "Cut it out." She shook her head. Said, *Weren't me.*
Then he felt it again. Said, *Well then, who the hell is it?*
He wanted to turn around. Tried. Couldn't. Roy Bentley
was never completely happy with being Roy Bentley,
the bastard son of a middle-aged woman of privilege but
sliding into shock treatments and sorrowful disintegration.
He wanted to be anyone but who he was, anyone not staring
toward this stationary phantom light. But forget the light.
Forget the habit of some vertebrates with opposable thumbs
to fashion grandiose fiction from what's true around them.
Forget that Edith wasn't the sharpest knife in the drawer.
Forget the stunned audience of two and a collective gasp
when the light went out. Forget that exhausted, dogged
persistence that occasionally wins out over failed marriage,
war, and bad luck anywhere but especially in Appalachia.
And remember this: They made it home, to Fleming-Neon,
by walking and swinging their arms and talking nonsense
in the dark until a dog barked and they ran, hearing a voice
like a memory of leaves rustling or their mother's voice;
the voice telling them, whatever else, not to look back.

## Letter from Eastern State Hospital, 1957

Her brother, D.V. Bentley, a doctor, arranged the commitment
for the misdemeanor offense of aiming and firing a .45 at a man,
my grandfather, Bob Beach, who abandoned her after promises.

The story is: she stayed angry, murderously so, for years after.
Twenty years—give or take a couple of months—behind walls.
The letter was signed *Very truly yours* by Logan Gragg, M.D.

Forget that 1957 was a boom year for everyone in Kentucky.
Forget long trains of coal from holes in the heart of the place.
Whatever they did to Susan Bentley there, my first memory

of my grandmother is of a woman so enraged she faced off
a child, gathering her arms against her bosom, saying, *What
in the hell are you looking at, you little son of a bitch?* We

were driving her back to the sanitarium. Neon to Lexington.
Maybe she didn't like that her son, my father, was guardian.
Maybe she hated that her hair—blue-black as a seam of coal,

shiny as the Big Sandy River when she went in to the hospital—
had turned the same gray as roadside snow. Whatever the case,
she turned her whole body at once. Like a statue on its plinth.

He kept the letter in an envelope with 6-cent Eisenhower
stamps—my father who expired in my arms, sliding down
into sheets the color of that ancient patient-history letter.

## Outside Lexington, Susan Bentley Decides
## She's Seen Enough of Sanitariums

For me, everything's a memory of electric shock.
May light spiders in a Model A's windshield
and I want to make lightning-bolt cracks
web across pastoral landscapes of horse farms—
so what if I'm rife with a Roman Empire
of maggots after that resettling of my vault
during the excavations for the Dollar Store.
If we're Spirit, and we are, you'll hear me out.

Once, in a bout of pure brokenheartedness,
I was Everywoman. The spring was one of those
you cried riding past it. There was an invocation
to the general lack of fairness in the slouch
of a summerhouse, the hum of abiding favor
in the spotted wings of a whole fritillary phylum
of insects. The air was like a song or scream,
terribly full. I added the weight of persona,

so when my brother said, "Stop your fidgeting"
and "Susan, don't make me stop this car"—
well, rather than say anything I leaned back
and planted both my low-heeled black shoes.
I kicked like I was putting out the fires of Hell.
Brother pulled to the side of US 60 West—
when he slapped me, I saw a Universe of stars
and whispered, to myself, so *so* many wishes.

## Wayne Whitaker Freezes Hope in the Sights
## of His Kentucky Long Rifle

From the photograph in *The Mountain Eagle*
titled GUNSMOKE, you know Wayne Whitaker
wears overalls and has a brother named Waylon.

The article says Wayne is a native of Hallie, Kentucky.
And in other news, a scandal sheet at Wayne's feet
says the human soul weighs $1/3000^{th}$ of an ounce.

What we don't see, beyond the gray-white billow,
is the other headline: ELVIS PICTURE WEEPS
and God's hand in this—how else could Wayne W.

have shot an impressively tight X and lost?
God, Thief of Harvests, Builder of the Stars,
has fixed the Mountain Heritage Black Powder Shoot.

That's what Wayne says in the article, adding
that God has whispered to his brother the teller
at the Mayking Christian Bookstore—

PO Box 400, Mayking, KY 41837—that Fleming-Neon
is where the trumpets will sound and Judgment Day
commence. Still, the way Wayne eyes the target,

showing us, in other photographs, what to do,
when and how to breathe hold move—
God could do worse than pull up a lawn chair

and bet on this $1/3000^{th}$ of an ounce
who may make shooters of us all
before the pig roast.

## Walking to Fleming Hospital

In the land where coal is king and queen there is a bar,
a big room where miners fight for something to do. Inside
is a framed image of Franklin Delano Roosevelt—
by the Men's Room where discerning Republicans spit,
though never at the face in the frame. Which is what I do.
Because he died, the President, and left me at the head
of a column of miners, striking miners, who faced down
an army that Harry S. Truman called out by executive order.
And so of course there's someone takes issue with my politics.
Someone "built like a brick shithouse," as they say. A giant.
The giant is just some unlucky miner who I don't see coming,
who has made his way past the barstools and two rows of tables
to land a first you'll-feel-that-tomorrow punch. Which I answer.
I'm holding my own until I hear *pop!* and then hear myself say,
*Sonofabitch shot me!* and *That damn Johnny Belcher shot me!*
Simple miracles, and most family myths, are made of walking
alone at night like this, and to a hospital where a pretty nurse
you went to high school with won't ask since she knows you,
knows the sort of man you are: how the Potters have done
their share of bar-fighting and dying in eastern Kentucky.
It's no miracle a man like me wants to live. Enough so
that he drags himself to assistance. Walks in, bleeding.
And I don't know when I collapse, but I'm on the floor
looking up into lights that pass for Heaven's gate and
then seeing the nurse hovering, her breasts like hills,
small white hills, the maybe-last-thing I'll likely see
as a consequence of hawking up and letting fly one
huge you-guessed-it in a dead president's direction.
I'd have preferred being shot over the pretty nurse
who asks for my next of kin as I whisper *Mary.*

## Plenty

*What is wrong with me, he thought. Plenty.*
*The land of plenty. The sea of plenty. The air of plenty.*

—Ernest Hemingway, *Islands in the Stream*

It has everything to do with fathers and mothers
and how, each day, they hand off disappointment
like lunch money or some caution about the world,
warning as innocuous as to watch crossing streets,
though they know their fears are never our fears.
Maybe because they are immigrants or outsiders,
isolates starting over in places that aren't home,
though they buy houses in neighborhoods where
CD players spin Frank Sinatra or Tony Bennett
and the food smells are a familiar slap in the face.
As their children, we are loved, if we are loved,
for as long as it takes to watch *Avatar* or *Titanic*
on a big-screen TV by a fireplace with fake logs
where there's heat but then nothing to show for it.
And if they believe in God, our beloved parents
wreathed in cigarette smoke and titanic self-doubt,
then that must be our God, especially since smoke
is a perfect metaphor for that which spirals outward.
When we love, later, as adults, they're in the room.
Women we choose are our mothers in unguarded
moments; men, a father's rage and something else.
If it has always been this way, then what excuse
could they fashion for not warning us, even once,
how nearly everything about this is myth? America,
all your bankruptcies are blockbuster 3-D movies
about the Rule of Law as the Law of the Jungle
in which bodies flit from tree to doomed tree,
a CGI starship or marvel of the White Star Line
brandishing a Stars & Stripes or a Union Jack.
It has been our bad luck to dream their dream.
We dream it yet. And if our kisses are fires,
they have been fed little for far too long—
they cool quickly, they taste like ashes.

## In Time All Will Be Green Again

In Dayton, Ohio, my mother previews a face in a passing car.
A car that shiny in '52 is about coal-country squalor. Escape.
My father parks in one of the metered spaces by the statuary
for a restaurant called Big Boy. He looks her way just once.
She waves by the chubby kid with a tray of cheeseburgers.

Their reunion might as well be a silent movie at the Neon,
a theater his uncle owns in a town by the same name: Neon.
Maybe *Birth of a Nation*, KKK on horseback. Burning crosses.
Maybe *City Lights* where America is at least better than that.
Back from a war in Korea, my father is divorced. His wife

had cheated. Gotten pregnant. Told him she'd been forced.
Mother will say, later, she took the bus to Dayton because
the Gem City isn't the end of the road Neon, Kentucky is.
Ohio in winter is gray—the sky, the grasses—but in time

all will be green again since there is work in Ohio.
Today, he asks her to a movie. And she isn't thinking
when she smiles and hugs him, then volunteers which
theaters have the best popcorn, the best fountain Cokes.
Row houses and hillsides resurrect as the light in his eyes.

## Elegy in November

My father had an uncle who was a doctor in Kentucky.
A few weeks before he died, that uncle survived a crash.
Uncle Doc (D.V.) was raising his voice to ambulance men,
telling them he was dead anyway. To take a couple of steps
back. My father told me D.V. sat up, having gone through
the windshield, safety glass in waves like corrugations
on an ocean. My father seemed to think that maybe
D.V. knew, then, there is no Hand of God in landing
in red-berried viburnum. That the mystery of survival
is inseparable from being, at all times, a cosmic puppet.
A marionette whose strings every so often get tangled
before falling right again in darkness or beneath lights.
The way he told the story you'd have thought he was
there. In the wreck. But he wasn't. Still, he just knew.
Like he knew D.V. to be the kind to decrypt bruises
in private. To define Impact as another life event—
on my father's last day I offered to fix eggs, but he
waved off talk of eating. He said he knew which bills
needed paid. Neither of us imagined I would hold off
paramedics the way Uncle Doc had, after the wreck,
then wait for the DNR to be driven from across town.
All that day, he had kept saying that he was tired, beat,
but the coal stove of his heart would glow red again—
maybe he wanted to hear a Southern accent; even mine,
which isn't much of one, according to the blood relatives
in Kentucky. From where I stood, it looked to be hard
to let go. And so I said, *Dad* and *Are you all right?*
That time, he sat up as if birds had returned with
spring; though it was November, a coughing fit,
which ended with him staring, an hour away yet.

# VII
New Poems

## My Mother's Red Ford

Even now, in some parking lot in the Afterlife,
it starts hard. Burns a quart between oil changes.
Even in the territory of the perfect and redeemed,

it needs new rubber—all four tires—a water pump.
Maybe an alternator. If any Galaxie 500 is a Ford
in this life, then so must it be in the life to come.

It's fifty years, but I still dream of packing the car
to run away and try our luck in New Mexico: four
adolescents panic-loading food blankets pillows,

the gargantuan trunk brimming with whatever fits.
She let me drive it, but I paid my insurance. Repairs.
My first love and I made out, once, in the front seat

at the drive-in. Big bench seat. Sometimes, now,
I'll see it, one like it, or think I do, and remember
my mother is another life that's kicked to the curb,

though it happens to all of us with enough miles
and wear in the wrong places. I like to imagine her
pulling up in that red two-door, hair to her shoulders,

Fats Domino or Nat King Cole or late-Elvis loudly
blaring from the AM radio as proof she'd survived
without a man. I love seeing her behind the wheel,

fast-waving her invitation for me to snap a picture.
Like she isn't disappointed being one of the dead
as long as she gets to go places in that car of hers.

## Distances of the Planets from the Sun

I'm on a field trip tonight, looking at the night sky
in the Dayton planetarium, a bright litter of galaxies
unspooling on a shared axis—I see my mother's face.
Years before anything terrible happened, not counting
a backwoods upbringing or my father's serial desertions.
Hair the color of open coal cars at close of day in the hills,
breath of stardust welling up from the Void, a furrow of care
between her eyes. See the face turn into a sag of lawn chairs.
See the celestial arabesques that the tour guide says are three
hundred fifty thousand light-years distant. Then: *give or take.*
One quadrant of blue, pleated with arroyos of nothingness,
mimics the face of the crucified Christ looking heavenward,
crying out, *My God, My God, why hast Thou forsaken me?*
Constellations buzz-hum *tsk-tsk* at the outline of his back,
the Christ, wavelengths of light not as quantifiable as love,
though nearly as measurable as the distances of the planets
from the sun. I'm pointing. Reminding myself "supernova,"
the word, stands for the force of nature who sent me money
for groceries: my mother. That dark sector is the time she
took five thousand dollars from me from the sale of the
house we shared on paper. Took it saying that she could.
Without tears. There, by Virgo, is the nanny she was
to Alice Stallard. There, the Nettie who sold real estate,
and a Nettie who rose every morning to breathe naphtha
and steam-crease sleeves and cuffs—as a hired girl. There
she is, made up in a box, a heart skilled in conditional love,
hovering like some ghost planet above a black-hole grave.

## Spirituals

I was twenty and just discharged from the Air Force.
My foot would hit that red steel pedal as if stepping on
the throat of Richard Milhous Nixon. I'd let up before
stepping again, the big Wabash press and me moving
in rhythm. My mission: not to lose focus and to put
two bends into an S of pipe. Pass it to the annealer.

At shift's end, and after a bit of mandatory overtime,
I ached as I had on hearing my first spiritual, Granny
Potter rocking as she sang it. Her voice enclouded like
the brushing-by of angel wings, the singing her proof
that we are more than bodies born to work and sleep
and then work some more. All I thought I wanted

was to come home to a Holly Park trailer and a wife.
Someone who could abide Ohio. Anneal the wounds
of having served. Maybe pronounce my name as if
*Roy* was a sweet sound to her. A woman with not
a lot of uncried tears if not outright joy to share.
That stamping press was a reliquary for black

rosaries of Hope. Once, an overhead line burst,
raining down hydraulic fluid that shoaled the floor.
It was tough to stand, but the work was what we had
instead of God or love of country and so you kept at it.
I can't say I heard anything in the machine resembling
Spirit unless you count the roar it made before it blew.

## The Cat Who Tried to Sleep at the Foot of the Deathbed of Abraham Lincoln

*for Cathy and Lee Martin*

What if William Petersen had a respectable mouser named
Abby and that quick, orange curve jumped onto the body.
What if Lincoln's oldest son Robert, arrived on the scene,

and attending to his mother, inconsolable Mrs. Lincoln,
had then considered the blood track and pawprint-record
across what Will Petersen offered to be put to good use—

thinking how his, Robert's, father prized animals, cats too—
commanded that Abby not be brushed aside but allowed
to keep returning through the night, scuttling underfoot,

a velvet approximation of a Virginia free as the slaves.
And so, the warm coins of the paws of a small live-thing
padded the bare-wood-to-carpet of a first-floor bedroom

across from Ford's Theater where men carried Lincoln,
men amazed at being asked to do that in the pouring rain.
Biographers agree they laid him, the president, diagonally

onto a four-poster where a cat was accustomed to lying,
furry ambler swept from bedclothes enough times, finally,
that it took to purring its grievance above muted voices.

# Buzz Aldrin, American Astronaut,
# Stands Next to the Stars & Stripes on the Moon

*for Christine Lysnewycz Kruk Holbert*

Neil Armstrong of Wapakoneta, Ohio is out of the shot.
This is Buzz and Old Glory. They'd killed our favorite

Irish-Catholic president. JFK. Taught him about riding
around in open Lincoln limos in Stetson-hatted Texas.

Cronkite is doing a voice-over. Same voice as that day
in Dallas when a whole world held its breath then wept.

By hopping around, Aldrin is affirming America's right
to swaddle the globe in the rhetoric of Manifest Destiny.

Nixon phones Apollo 11 live and in prime time, so Buzz
stops moving, though it's his show and remarkable terrain.

Supposedly, he is trying not to upstage the presidential call.
Not to say what any Presbyterian elder might, having given

himself holy communion from a secret kit he stowed away.
This moonscape could be the slow-changing light of Kyiv,

a bullying Russian-winter a harvest of unhappiness, hunger.
Over Aldrin's shoulder, it's a desperate planet: Golda Meir

is down there asserting the rights of the State of Israel over
Palestinians; consenting to sanctioned killings which, when

taken together, make a nation. Go ahead, Buzz. Bust some
goofy dance move like it's the first sock hop on the moon.

## Rebel Rebel

I'm back from the Air Force. Bend pipe for Fords.
And I will be the talk of the town since I'm twenty
and picking up a seventeen-year-old at high school.

I pull in, park, the V-8 idle an audible *yes, oh yes*.
She likes my Firebird and that I like David Bowie.
Says she hates Ohio worse than a visit to a dentist,

worse than when she fractured her forearm in a fall,
though she confesses to still loving trees. Climbing.
The night we met I was lip-synching Neil Diamond

and telling everyone that he was born in Brooklyn.
I was drunk and loud-stupid in the way that some
young men are. She liked me. I drove her home

and we watched a huge maple surrender leaves
in the dark. I kissed her and then she kissed me.
I see she has sewn *Roy & Joey* and an arrowed

heart into her motorcycle jacket. I'm waiting
as she runs to meet me, the jacket belt flapping
against insurgent leather. I get out and wave.

I'm a string-puppet, a kind of love marionette.
Already, at 17, this one knows about rebellion.
Says that her chief-master-sergeant father says

it's a consequence of who we expect not to fail
failing us. I know he means the world we trust.
Like the branch she told me had seemed sturdy

then wasn't and she heard someone screaming.
She fights with a load of substantial textbooks.
*Introductory Biology* is sliding from her arms.

# AWOL on the Fourth of July

> *It was my way of breaking free. I was anything but history.*
> *I was the wind.*
>
> —Joy Harjo, "Running," *The New Yorker*

At nineteen, I was one hundred and eighty pounds of Crazy
and fired up that sweet-sounding 350 V-8 and pulled out

of the barracks lot, staying within the on-base speed limit.
At the gate, Air Police stared before waving me through.

I was sick inside about some things, though I'd be lying
if I said anything but that it felt great, saying Fuck you

to nineteen seventy-three and the Illinois military town
where even the corn at roadside stood at parade rest.

There are heroes from those times, but I wasn't one.
I shoved in an 8-track of Gregg Allman, then steered

south toward the fireworks at the drive-in off Illinois 45.
That time, I turned around somewhere near Indianapolis.

I was practicing, trying to find out how far I could get on
a payday-fat wallet, a few changes of clothes, and Attitude.

At nineteen, I was a glutton for music. Something to smoke.
Miles of asphalt and signage that read as *The Book of Lives.*

Nixon was president. If America was one big military town
that hates itself, then why not see what a good GM engine

will do in country in love with the reek of black powder
wafting by on night skies of downward-drifting light.

## The Spell for Stopping Those Who Take Everything

A promised job in New Jersey sent us home
with nothing to buy a house but my VA loan.
For her, stories were proof of wounding at the

hands of her wheelchair-bound mother or funny
in the way her father's joke about a "can of pee"
and a canopy bed is somewhat amusing. Once.

One story was of a sister pinning her to the floor
under a dangle of saliva meant to tease. Trust me,
to bully. Look closely. See if you aren't visioning

the thick cord of spittle fake-launched. Launched.
Lonely is the child and lovely are the russet eyes
flashing as she raises a slurry of damning spells.

I'd like a spell for those who took everything.
Once, in Wisconsin; then, in Florida where we
loved sun, the starry dark as surprising as a

dropped handkerchief. No one gets out what
they put in. It's not even close. Nevertheless,
sooner or later, they'll pin you down. Spit.

## As Fallible as Angels

Like a river in a time of dryness or drought
the stream of Imagination (mine at least)

was cracked path for nothing of consequence
until George Kosta sauntered up our street

with explanations about Sex. In Ohio in 1965
the spectacular catastrophe of his pronunciation,

*mis*pronunciation, of words for the male and female genitalia
was like the vision of a dog with one good eye.

His parents were from Greece and his T-shirts carried
garlic histories, the smells of his mother's dim kitchen;

Mr. Kosta's hair, Vitalised, glowed like black sunshine,
and Mrs. Kosta was round, ample-breasted.

George knew his life to be like a bridge he was driving over
in a borrowed car, a finned Fairlane with the windows

rolled down, all that wheel-humming a story of rivets.
He knew what it takes to make the crossing into

country you've let deep into your immigrant heart like hope.
And he said his father had lectured him, saying,

"It's a *pen-us*" and "It's a *vag-unuh*" and so, at 11, it was.
For as long as we lie in the grass, looking up,

waiting for a streetlight in the shape of a cock to challenge
a heaven of night sky as Mediterranean-dark as olives.

## Oahu Theory

Waimea Bay is water over reefs until we recall
the last wish of the drowned is for land. An hour
silvering down as cold wet air. At the foliate edge
of the Pacific, what will not finish is a constant—

an ellipsis of crest and trough, crest and trough.
One theory is that the starlight-and-DNA is so
misused by those wanting to lie down and die

that many of the dead habitually petition to return.
If the premise is that the Beautiful nixes Suffering,
this isn't that. This is light and wave as grieving:
half a Shakespearean play, half the soliloquies

and stage-directions of surviving on an island.
And islanders wish only to be left alone to see
to real estate prices, a full moon looking back

on homelessness with roots in Eden (to judge
by the noisy epidemic of feral chickens). Still,
here, to exist is to wake constantly beside water
where a day will, and may, start with lovemaking

that relieves the lovers of everything and nothing.
It can come as no surprise, then, that any number
of stars are like mica-points over a night ocean.

## The Leaping Cat's Human Assistant

If you wanted to know what it's like, guiding
a 400-pound Siberian tiger's sovereign glide path,
positioning hoops of flame or a pedestal, covering
for the random poor disposition of quadrupeds,
afterwards in his silver trailer would be the place.
You'd carry in categorical praise like a drunk friend
you came by to pour into bed. If he asked you in,
and you sat, a spiral notebook opened on your lap,
one of those micro-recorders ready to take down
what you miss tracing a fine-veined facial scarring,
a line of suture marks like the fletching of an arrow,
evidence of implicit trust, he'd likely be no talker.
Gone quiet perhaps, he'd point to the snow outside.
An ease of fall through the aisles of tree branches
or the carnival-bright particulars of a room lit
by the bald indifferent glow of a rent-a-sign.
You would want, in his own words, the camber
of feral shoulders at the animal height of each jump,
the way he ritually checks off what is about to happen
in an incremental three- or four-step "drop"—which,
he says, another reporter compared to a pro quarterback.
Circular trailer windows would bleed resonant veins
of snowmelt, an embroidered velvet throw-pillow
reverse-reflecting the phrase *Panthera tigris altaica.*
He'd wave you to walls of circus posters, memorabilia.
All business, you'd begin: *How did you acquire the cat?*
He'd thieve tumblers from a kitchenette pass-through.
Set the glasses on a table. If you were attractive, his type,
or lucky—you don't have to know tigers to know luck—
he might pour you some of what he was having. "We
grew up together," he'd say, opening a bottle of Scotch.
An epithalamium of dark liquor would leap to glasses.

## Whole Lotta Shakin' Goin' On

First off, you're in an off-duty cabbie's Chevy. In the front seat.
A fogbound field is boundary. Through a windshield, night hovers.
He's said that *that* bus doesn't run anymore, but he'll get you there.
He's failed, he says, to make clear the fare for the thirty-mile trip.
Seems not to care this is your first full day after military service.
Of course you would have done better to have started walking.
In an air-force-issue duffle of civvies you thought to pack:
a Swiss army knife on the floor at your feet. An open blade
you may want to use to answer the unsolicited stroking of a leg.
Maybe you like that "Whole Lotta Shakin' Goin' On" is playing,
but you're a brittle glide of youth after the bus ride. Dazed-numb.
And when you say *Fuck no*, he reaches under a seat as if for a gun.
The air here, it's like breathing loss or defeat if they gave off fumes.
You exit the car *in media res* and hit road surface like a bag of hope
for better. In addition to sacrificing a field jacket, the knees of your

Levis, a lot of flesh, you roll like the postal sack of Stupid you are.
What you see, picking yourself up, is the noisy orchestral motion
of grackles settling onto the power lines. Engines rev in the gullet
of dawn. Storefronts glow mostly with the light we see emitted
from stars. You drag yourself and the duffle to a field. Lie flat.
Somewhere down this road you rise to walk, your parents die.
When they die, your folks, you travel back here because they
were there for you on nights like this, saying what they said
and given that often, in Ohio, any victory is a pyrrhic one.
If excess of grief is any kind of crime, it's a misdemeanor.
You'll walk into an empty house. The beds will be there.
One your mother read herself to sleep in before she died.
The double with that sawn-level place in the footboard,
cherished furniture your pops marked as a consequence
of roughhousing in the world he was young in once.

# On the Deck of the Spokane, 1994

Another purplish blue Seattle dawn after a week of cold and grey,
the plain truth of winter on the far-off hillsides across Puget Sound—

I think of Gloria Regalbuto, and the approaching end of the ferry ride,
"never seen anything like this," she enthuses, "and the stars last night . . ."

then points to the stenciled PLEASE, KEEP OFF THE LADDER sign
beside the wrought-iron ladder I'm holding onto. She raises a camera

and steps forward from the painted railing into the unrecoverable Now
underneath the cacophonous squeakings and squealings of shore birds

whose wings churn chill, sea-rank March air. She says, Be yourself,
but means for me to be perfectly still in this the hour after first light.

She is looking straight at me, waving directions, and leading me out
from a furl-of-wings-as-trapezoidal-shadow that has fallen across us.

Like the stars she says she saw as for the first time, the birds overhead
are moving in a space above the jacketed man and companion-traveler,

map-wielders evolved from deoxyribonucleic acid asparkle with injury
and forfeiture, one of them framed by the stenciled name of the ferry—

someone the other knows now as a story of a ferry ride at winter's end.
Someone she has seen dressed in the uniforms of morning and midday

and evening, a man with no regrets unless you count choice of clothing.
Someone who made an unplundering mad dash beside her to the wharf

and onto a boat smelling of salt air and mud-earth, through a turnstile,
up some stairs, having surrendered to hope that love will get us there.

Ghost-stars and the shore birds beat against the tines of their cages
of sky. At least one other stranger nods, then she takes the picture.

## Belmont Auto Theatre

We were more than the best story of the place
but less than infinities of light falling on bodies.
More than the history of the 1903 Wright Flyer.
In love with Richard Burton and Liz Taylor in
*Cleopatra* or *Who's Afraid of Virginia Woolf*,
what better use for botched orchards? Why

not truck in gravel and regrade that acreage?
Having escaped like Wilbur and Orville Wright
who accomplished their first figure eight nearby,
my Kentucky parents fled famishment to drown
in vague regret as mists skidded across a moon
not yet flecked with American flags. In 1966

you drove up to the awninged ticket booth
and said something, the way my pops would
before opening his wallet, the air-conditioning
receding in a rush. **Belmont Auto Theatre**
in red and black tube neon on the street-
facing side of the screen. On the speakers.

On speaker poles pointing skyward forever.
A shadow-name scuffed car hoods. Reversed
in the windshields of Fords Chevys Plymouths.
If I come back after death it will be as the angel
of memory circling above bright acres where
there will soon be sufficient dark to begin.

## Ohio Birth

*after Susan Mitchell*

No barge traffic blackens the Ohio this morning.
Rivermen chop the ice from wharves, but nothing
is moving when it's this cold. There are trucks. Buses.
And the diesel-stink on the black-and-white Dayton air—
if the 1950s had been a woman, she would have smoked.
Been repetitively reaching for an L & M filter cigarette.

I'm about to be born in a hospital named for a guy—
an anonymous traveling worker—who stopped to help.
On a main road between Damascus and Jerusalem,
according to the King James Version of the Bible
my grandmother Potter will be reading to me, nightly.
A white Jesus might as well be leaning against the sliding

glass of the stork logo-ed Good Samaritan Hospital nursery.
In a moment my mother will ask to hold me. In a moment
I will be lifted from my polypropylene bassinet, my blue-
for-Boy blanket trailing. Later, I am lifted from a place
at a table in the dining room of our house in Kettering.
What does my first-time mother know, coming around,

except she wants to sleep. She thinks whatever she thinks.
And it's none of our business. Because you had to be there,
and a woman. Recitations I'm about to hear concern hellfire.
To a kid: like having your hair combed with burning briquettes.
I am so young the messages beat into my brain like the stories
of my birth in which my mother plays herself and isn't brave.

## Spirit Recordings

*Machines lent an air of scientific respectability to their claims.*
*They promised a purer, seemingly less corruptible connection*
*with the dead. You can't trust a human not to fake ectoplasm*
*out of sheep lung, but you ought to be able to trust a machine.*

—Mary Roach, *Spook*

In 1926, Dr. Neville Whymant tried to authenticate
a phonograph recording of the voice of Confucius.
The ancient Chinese philosopher spoke through
George Valiantine, a medium, whose only visible
means of support was to be a vessel for the Dead.
(The Dead, it turns out, are a lot of very famous
souls loitering around.) Dr. Whymant concluded:
*Though it is possible that you might hallucinate*
*people, you could not hallucinate a gramophone.*

If discarnates speaking directly through mediums
and spirit guides like Sabbatini, the Italian tenor
who turned up at a Cape Town séance in 1930—
via the pirated vocal cords of Mrs. T. H. Butters:
recorded belting out a hypermasculine "Pagliacci"—
and if the postmortem voices of Mohandas Gandhi
and Oscar Wilde and the Archbishop of Canterbury
may be said to take the place of one last true look
at Existence, then let all those listening decipher

the kind of June morning when rain won't stop
and voices conjure a heart that has much to do
with what we mean by saying the word *God.*
It seems the truly lonely are all true believers.
Break out the latest Psychic Telephone. Get
the medium as far from the room as you like.
That's a white inflatable rubber bladder attached
to a blue transmitter and a pair of red headphones.
That's me: shouting to be heard over Sabbatini.

## Texas History

On the Texas side of the river in 1972,
there were Mexican children everywhere.
And for as long as they granted us leave,
the air force, we were men among them.
The kids were the streets of San Antonio,
in Bexar County, the city telling itself lies
in two languages: one that America cares,
the other, that war is how we show a love
of country. We were not in our Class As;
we were in civvies in search of a woman
who wore tolerance for men like tie-dye.
In honor of stupidity and the far-off war,
my story walked next to theirs, the many
who spoke Spanish and a halting English
salted with loud laughter and overlooking,
faces bent enough to be hard to make out
in movie theaters with their dim lighting:
families of women with several children,
their fathers elsewhere. Working. Gone.
Sometimes the story is someone else's.
Sometimes it's the way of small bodies
restless and turning in their wild mercy
to declare how this world is without us.
That year, though I couldn't know it yet,
and in honor of all that we leave behind
unreplaced, I learned the Spanish word
*injusticia*. Sometimes it's a smiling child
whose language skills reduce to pointing
and asking why you're the color you are.
Sometimes it's the story of how you felt
in a Texas audience of brown kid-faces
that anoints you with the oils of failure.

## Approaching Seattle

On a ferry my son Scott, a boy of 8, rides on deck
in a Sonics jersey and shorts. It's warm for December,
unseasonably so. Starless night-sky slides overhead.
He works the toggle of a Gameboy. The Emerald City
glows with strings of seasonal lights. And the *Chief
Seattle* makes a Rorschach blot of the breaking water.

Fifteen years later, he sends an email to let me know
that he walked on the Great Wall: *One of those things
where pictures do not do it justice. Unbelievable.*
The email, dated the 5th of July, says he celebrated
the 4th on Chinese streets and is still feeling it:
*Drank a lot of Budweiser, ate a hamburger.*

He says that he got stuck in an expat bar for a while.
It had rained; the street flooded. He uses *monsoon*
to describe the suddenness and force of the drenching.
Locals sent paper boats with lighted candles in them
across Sanlitun Street: *which had become a river.*
Nineteen ninety-three is held-breath in the photograph

as he looks to his right to assure himself that no one
is following. (No one was, though someone had walked
over, just, and tapped his small shoulder.) The score, then,
was what he said it was. Now, it's what we tell ourselves
that must vanish like a garish glow of Christmas lights
or all that engine-smoke trailing the ferry like memory.

This is my boat to you, Scott: a poem wicked and lit
with the universal forces of blood and breath crossing
a blur of time zones to say, in your words: *I'd never
been so excited about the fourth of July as yesterday.
My first one out of the country. Ended up singing
"The Star-Spangled Banner" at the top of my lungs.*

*American Landscape with Boys in a Car*


The year: 1971. The destination: Santa Fe, New Mexico.
The car was a '64 Ford Galaxie. Lipstick-red with red interior.
Bench seats and an AM radio. Bald tires. Signature circular
taillights with the chrome centers that were hard to wax.
Who could predict we'd get the opportunity—my parents
at a funeral hundreds of miles from Ohio, in Kentucky—
to steal the car and go tearing ass out of The Buckeye State?
I thought the first night would go on forever, but it lasted
as far as the Illinois State Line where we slept and woke
before dawn and read maps by a dome light. What I remember
of the second day is getting to Route 66 then Route 66 rattling past
like strings of boxcars—the radio on and Rod Stewart singing
"Maggie Mae" over the voices of first one then another high-school
truant promising *I'm game for never going back if you are.*
By the second night we were so scared we couldn't sleep.
And I remember the pleather seat stuck to me with my shirt off.
The third day the road pulled us like a hipflask from a pocket
while James Taylor sang "You've Got a Friend" over the bullshitting,
what boys do to avoid talking about what it is that bothers them.
All that May morning, what kept us going were the changes
in landscape—west Texas was no Ohio, and New Mexico
was this latitude longitude of magical realism: desert foliage
and the beginnings of mountains the color of lips brushing sky.
I'm sure I wanted to kiss Adventure full on the mouth, we all did.
At four-thirty in the afternoon that day, we drove into Santa Fe.
We couldn't see home in the Spanish architecture or the faces
of those who stared if they even looked at us, so we called home.
They told us to turn around and we pointed the Ford north, stopping
at the boyhood home of Mark Twain, at Lincoln's Springfield house,
checking off the fear of being someone to whom nothing ever happens.

## Dayton

In the 1950s in Ohio,
there were jobs. Affordable housing
and a life on wide, new streets
lit not so much by grievance
as untranslatable infatuation with future.
Nouns verbs adjectives in stories
in *The Saturday Evening Post* hummed
with expectation for America as a republic
where indifference to suffering was sin
and sin sent you to Purgatory or Hell.
That America was magnanimous—
there was the matter of an opaque past
of unspeakable wholesale suffering,
but millions were rescued from poverty
by union-wage jobs assembling widgets—
and synonyms for prosperous
endlessly tripped off the tongue.
However, as Jesus said once, the poor
will take the heart out of you if you don't look
away. There was baseball. Color television.
Cars with fins. And 25-cent a gallon gasoline.
Never mind what they tell you, the goal
was to consume *everything*. The motto
on the currency should have been In Us
We Trust. I hear the past is uninhabitable,
unambiguous in a complicity to oppress.
True. But the sky over that Dayton
with its scandal of exhaust—that sky
welcomed kids out into a day. And rain
on Saturdays washed us clean a while.
There was an after-music to laughter.
Why doubt the world is gorgeous?

## Minuteman Missile

In the 20ᵗʰ Century my father loved his government job:
maintaining the well-calibrated heart of the nuclear arsenal.
He said, *We can put one of those babies through a window
in the Kremlin after a 6000-mile flight. We made that here.*
And, come Memorial Day, at the open house at the air base,
he'd show me his workbench in the cleanroom where dust
held its breath. Later, he might have almost nothing to say.
Maybe: *Keep it down. I'm watching fucking 60 Minutes.*

How he grew to love Minuteman missiles, the stockpile
whose reliable lethality he'd chosen to take ownership of.
Meaning, he thought about the consequences of the work.
Maybe he had the moral compass of a death camp guard,
but I loved that he sharpened the blade for the American
guillotine. That he visualized ICBMs unzipping the sky.
The hum and verdict of oscilloscopes was in his voice
when he said, You think about things *way* too much.

## He Spent a Year Hallucinating Peace

and, according to *The National Enquirer*, another
week and a half tossed in like pennies into a fountain.
The next day the murders began. The first of the waves

of new-dead and disfigured to be posed before detectives
who had lost their hard edge, meaning they choked up.
Imagine the exhalations from the body of the planet

under skies canopying the relinquishing of anger,
cloud cover giving way to blue notional brightness.
Even in Florida, husbands might've refrained from

dismembering wives, though random gunfire might
have kept up throughout west Texas like foreplay.
I see peace as my best day on the earth continuing.

I think of the nesting eagles atop a dead-oak flagpole.
I see flags of wings beating against bodies, featherfalls,
the comings and goings by first light in March in Ohio.

I want to believe the hatchlings can survive whatever.
I will open a door in the hotel of my hallucinations
if you will open a door in yours and invite me in.

## Architectures of Windfall

He's eight, traveling by train for the first time.
Buys a pack of Beemans. Opens a Superman comic.
Now he looks out at dead-of-winter fenced Ohio farms.
From the window seat, snowdrifts blur by at a fast walk,
then faster, blinding sun melting ice from the backs of hills.
The air outside is a flesh of snowflake and blowing snow,
countryside the red-tailed hawk circles in search of food.
He spits out an exhausted wad of Beemans. Deposits it
on the floor under a seat ahead. Unwraps another stick.
Behind him, a man and woman mouth words. The car
shudders gently. Clark Kent stammers word-balloons
for a skinny Lois Lane who turns on her spiked heels,
storming off as any irate traveler between destinations
would. Alone, the boy makes sense of the light of midday
as it pours into the car in the lull between frame-by-frame
battles wherein Evil bests Good until it doesn't, the crimson
S brightest of all the colors of the rainbow world. He sees
the flayed hedges of Auglaize County and Wapakoneta
as a glare and glint of February entering the secular air.
The unimaginable gladness of the yet-to-be-disappointed
is in the compartment in the person of an 8-year-old boy—
bent shoulders, too-heavy head, architectures of windfall
idoling in a window as skybright barns, unplowed roads,
the occasional covered bridge over ice-fletched waters.
The Daily Planet might as well be the Masonic Temple.
Clark Kent and Lois Lane might as well be from Dayton
and on their way to Lima, might as well be holding hands
and happy. Like a man and woman the next aisle over
who whisper as they look out at the trees skeletoned
by shadows like an x-ray of what lives, what dies.

## Wild Monkeys to Measure Radiation Levels in Fukushima

> *Dosimeters are extremely sensitive instruments. Although they are constructed for rugged use, they should receive the same care as a wristwatch. Since dosimeters are hermetically sealed at the factory, they cannot be repaired or adjusted in the field. Therefore, if instrument malfunctioning is experienced, the instrument should be returned to the factory or your dealer. Dosimeters may be maintained in operating condition simply by cleaning the eyepiece lens and the charging switch insulator with clean water and a cloth that is free of lint and grit. Make sure the charging switch insulator is absolutely free of lint and moisture at all times. Caution: Do not insert any sharp objects into, or tamper with parts in the charging switch recess. Irreparable damage may be done.*
>
> —Arrow-Tech website

No banana dangled from 12-pound test fishing line, just a collar
tethered to the animal. No remote-controlled shocks to the gonads,
just a pastel-pink dosimeter by Arrow-Tech secured by Velcro.
One of the Japanese rad techs must have visited dosimeter.com
in the course of a dive and grab for solutions. He may have read,
in italic type, *Protection begins with Detection* and was sold.

These aren't lab monkeys coaxed from jungle-gym sanctuaries.
These are the heart humming where-are-the-tame-she-apes kind.
So my money is on the shaggy, Buddha-bellied simians resisting.
I picture a little Jedi-knight acrobatic trickster thwarting our efforts
at every just-in-time turn, the latest in a series of abject failures
of collective best intentions why we need to recruit him at all.

It's Christmas, so let me make you a present of this caution:
Next time you hear some co-worker blurt out *We could drop
wild macaques with dosimeter collars into the Hot Zone*—
beat it the hell out of there. Grab your lab coat and Thermos.
Disappear into the indigo night of not-knowing and not-saying.
The truth about how stupid we are is gaining on you. I'd say, Run.

## "Dream Caused by the Flight of a Bee Around a Pomegranate a Second Before Awakening"

*Salvador Dali painting*

Bengal tigers from the mouth of a single fish.
Ferocity grandly present mid-leap above a figure—
the white-skinned Sleeping Woman. Both breasts
are light-anointed as she floats over a bed of stone.
Above her, the tigers charge. In a world drawn from
this one, Dali is saying, she would do well to be awake.
Maybe the figure is someone the artist wants or would
like to take a bite out of. Perhaps beasts will devour
her alabaster perfection in a series of vicious gulps,
rendering her part of themselves and some cycle
of satisfying hunger under a white hint of moon—
as if perfection and ferocity were the same thing
and might as well be a rifle with its fixed bayonet
touching the tender inside of a raised right arm.
A wheat-gold horizon says the hour stares back
upon itself as an hour must, given half a chance.

What of the elephant on appendage-stilts, walking
a tideless ocean, a single pedestaled monument
its cargo as it halts in mid-step and trumpets?
A bee around the smaller of the pomegranates
is the reason for her dream, or so we are told.
Never mind the pomegranate's rubied promise.
Never mind that we are drawn to the elephant.
Dali knows a little about elephants, bees, fun—
if that bee is anything but a bee I'd be astonished.
And women wearing nothing are emblematic, sure.
The hereditary instructions written down in DNA.
But this one is Innocence and the message that
after the grand show of nucleotides and nebulae,
of droplets suspended between heavens and seeds
likewise suspended, there is what's left over. It
might as well be flesh. It might as well be love.

## Lost Storyline from The Life of the Flying Man

When all we have are limits, we live to exceed them
knowing the precincts of thin air are pathless, infinite.
Performing is like that, free of limitation or nearly free.
And who doesn't love a circus? All of us die, but a lucky
handful are alive and recognize it reaching for the bar,
which is where it should be after a triple with a twist.

The aerialist recalls a woman, a night of candle glow
and waiting for the dishes to be cleared away at last.
But the dishes stayed on the table and little was said
until a grand sweeping motion prepared—*Presto!*—
a serviceable place for the two of them to climb on.
The wreck of the world-at-hand is a thing to behold.

Who'd have thought the Palm Reader lusted after
the Flying Man? To be this fellow takes great hands.
Tolerance for the hard self-lecture and hurt of discipline.
And a second sense about what can drag a body down.
Where is she now? he wonders and rubs his callouses,
palms and fingers with thought processes of their own.

In the here and now, memory produces her obituary
and membership in the no-longer-traveling circus
of the dead. Novices, trying to be birds, somersault
then drop into netting like Spandexed eggs. An army
of clowns sweeps up by a slit in the pleated canvas
under signage extolling Exit in eye-catching red.

Where is forgiveness? Climbing into a clown car that
by any law of ergonomics comfortably fits but one.

## Four Torch Juggling—Kettering, 1965

I'd like to believe it began unaccountably
with playfulness and not because butternuts
littered a schoolyard where Joanie Prentice
invited me to watch her turn ten cartwheels
in a row in a dress. After that, I practiced
lofting serial tennis balls, fruit, Frisbees,
the pins from a Flintstones bowling set.

Anything taken to the brink is miraculous.
For hours, I pressed objects up into the air.
I went from balls and rings to what's called
"a three-sixty with pins" then on to dowels.
I wicked the dowels with old army belts.
I made backyard laundry lines luminous
with behind-the-back blind catches.

Once, I came close to calling it quits
after getting doused in a *whoof* of flame.
But I thought if she saw these lit wings
behaving exaltedly—and below a moon
the color of her hair—she'd likely applaud
and give me what I was trying to deserve,
what the cartwheels seemed to promise.

When the Cubans moved in across the street,
neighbors pronounced them "gypsies".
But old man Reager saw what I could do.
He wagged his head and called me over.
He read the burns, said *Quit the circus.*
It sounded like there would be girls along
to tell my fortune and make it come true.

## This Is Not a Dark Ride

A carny lowers the safety bar on a coaster car
I'm about to ride with my sons, at Kings Island
near Cincinnati, and I await my chance at joy,
though the idea of exalted futures ruins kings
and island-kingdoms of the heart. I'm listening
to a ballad about romance by Bruce Springsteen.
New Jersey is the subject of the song, a place

another singer says is like Ohio, only more so.
There is a silver carload of longing to listening
to loud rock 'n roll while your pregnant wife
leans over an amusement-park railing, smiling,
waving as she sets aside your latest indiscretion
by saying to herself, *At least he loves his kids*—
Matt, child-happy in that most ordinary of ways,

a 7-year-old staring out beyond the drop-off,
fearless, expectant; Scott, 3 the previous April,
asking a brother everything he can't ask a father.
Sherry, just beginning her pregnancy, won't be
riding with us. "Got in a little hometown jam,"
the song says, coming right out and recounting
everyone's recent past. Mine, for sure. A girl

in the car ahead of us shouts *We're moving!*
as if whatever else we thought would happen
the song of the chain-and-track mechanism
is breaking news, her *Oh, shit!* a revelation.
I think of that coaster ride sometimes now,
now that I know how a day can become heat
and complaining kids, and Disappointment,

now that my life after has broken my heart,
though I chose each twist and turn myself.
I bounced until I prayed, a student of bliss,

getting it, for which any rock 'n roll song is
a how-to: *Teaching the World to Say Yes.*
Like the sign said: This Is Not a Dark Ride.
Nor is it the story of learning to expect less.

*Fisher*

The rusted Can't Miss trap sounds sharply
overhead in the drop ceiling
on the average of once an evening all summer,
springs so stiff, action so old,
that when the balled Velveeta does its work
it is to catch mice alive, by a leg
or tail most often, trap retrieved
with the animal in it, kicking.
*But I used 3-in-1,* Virgil says, listening,
mopping sweat. Virgil Horsley,
fiftyish, alcoholic, a man etched
in hairline strokes of dismantlement,
used to be a preacher, Southern Baptist.
*Being justified freely by his grace*
*through the redemption that is in Christ Jesus.*
He drinks Scotch now and sits like a Judas
fond of a Lucky-Strike noose of smoke—
on the porch of a rented house. Thinks
of again signing on with the shrimp boats.
Fisher of mice, he thinks, settling back,
no breeze. Come fall he could go north,
to Ohio: one of the families he used to oversee.
He'd drink on credit at the Holiday Inn,
feast on home cooking. He'd have to hear
how he needed a job, his whole life made over:
*who against hope believed in hope.*
The hound out back bays in the heat.
A rooster a house over crows.
Last season, on the shrimp boats,
the sea breaking, he overcame the droning
in his head: a dull benediction not unlike singing.
*For as by one man's disobedience many were made sinners,*
*so by the obedience of one shall many be made righteous . . .*
After the long day's hauling in,
he could hear the white, threading waves

and think them water. Not the upraised
arms of supplication, earned fall, every leap
of faith a crowning. Across roof beams,
mice move overhead in heat and dark:
sudden springings to play at the air.

# Radio Nowhere

## 1. America, the Word

It rolls off the tongue like a straight razor
being fished from the pocket of an immigrant.
A last resort, it's deadly in the right hands.

Talking bad about a country is like running down
the dead or God, never a good idea, but America
is so synonymous with human blood flowing
through the streets of foreign countries, these days,
that one has to speak. If this place were a bird,

it would keep the curve of its flight a secret
(even from itself) for as long as it could, out of habit—
whatever part of the light leaked from its wings
would be redefined not as light but as something else:
*Senator, it depends on your definition of light* . . .

And when it was clear that this was one sick bird,
a carrier of not-so-exotic diseases like greed,
then they would turn out to sing an anthem
to its caterwaul of a history bursting in air
above a murmurous night surf's susurrus.

Likely, a shout would go up. *What a bright
and fugitive beast she is!* someone would say.
And: *Oh, but she is a pretty bird, isn't she?*

## 2. Radio Nowhere

Maybe it's a gift, the autumnal brown of botanicals,
tangles of washed-out-yellow palm fronds reminiscent

of deciduous trees in fall anywhere in the Buckeye State,
but the operation of light in South Florida's backyards

is about resignation: resigning oneself to blaring rap music
and the occasional shave-and-a-haircut car horn from US 1,

the fact that the Beautiful is, sooner or later, asphalted over.
Newsprint-colored sandy soil of development green space

shares the future of a recently-cleared acre now dotted
with small red pennants to mark where conduit went in.

Not that it matters all that much—the rich prosper here;
they root and grow and take over like nuisance plants

or retirees. No stopping them. In a windowed house
a white-robed man stands before a TV. Onscreen,

a flickering Bruce Springsteen is dressed in black.
Maybe he's mourning the state of his stupid country;

maybe he likes black in the way Johnny Cash liked black.
Maybe NBC will discover the thin line between greed

and greatness and fill the rest of us in on the epiphany.
Right. Maybe Matt Lauer is about to announce, live,

his opposition to the war in Iraq. Springsteen nods
in the direction of Tim Russert and Meredith Vieira,

then sings, *This is Radio Nowhere. Is there anyone*
*alive out there? This is Radio Nowhere*

## The Last Remaining Farm in the New Suburb

*for Gary Laberman*

One year before Sputnik, before JFK,
on the first afternoon of summer break
from Kettering, Ohio's public schools,
my grandmother Potter said not to spend all day
up the hill and in the orchard beyond
because, well, just because. My mother
had given instructions, I was sure. June apples,
the yellow-skinned fat variety, begged stealing
and so I was off—which means I'd died
to the world of the new suburbs we lived in
and had gone to Heaven-as-an-Orchard.
Down the hill, before the window air-conditioner,
I knew my grandmother's flatware fork would
pat loaves she signed with the whites of eggs.
I knew she sucked hard candy while she cooked.
I knew she suffered, with or without air conditioning.
I was with the workers of Ohio, by a rail line
so ancient even locals had forgotten its name.
I watched migrants fill and empty bins into crates
and stack the crates into trucks; I scented apples
and truck exhaust all day. By nightfall my stomach
ached from hunger, and I knew to head home
before the light failed. Across wood-and-wire
fences, again in Kettering, I remember the birds
sort of singing me on, the chirr of insects. I recall
the drawl-inflected notes of my name *(Rowee!)*
and raising both arms in the waist-high grasses.
I believe in love and expect to see it reappear
as a gaunt, aproned woman snatching weeds
from the sod. Straightening herself as I run up
and start talking, going on and on since I have
so much to say about how I've missed her.

## Waiting to Close the Station

In the lift-bay the best thing, by far,
is the smell of solvents and gasoline.
You don't have to be an adult to love it.
You don't have to shove your Shell ballcap
and head under the raised hood of an Impala,
adjusting a carburetor for the umpteenth time.
You don't have to wave to men with names
like Delbert or Junior and yell *Give it gas!*
You don't have to swear and toss a shop rag.
You could be a boy out of school, in 1961,
the owner's son. Your job: to stay the hell
out of the way until your father, the Roy of
Roy's Shell, says, "I'll tell you: *Hit the gas*
and you hit the gas, then let off and wait . . ."
You don't have to pound the steering wheel
and turn up the volume on the car's radio,
Ricky Nelson crooning "Hello Mary Lou"
or "Travelin' Man," which you loved then,
though not as much as the scent of gasoline
or being allowed to stay up past midnight.
Here comes the pump bell, from the dark,
signaling that tires are again rolling over it,
the hose, and bell-sounds from the islands
as someone dispenses a tankful of regular
or high-test, adding to a fat wad of bills.
And here's the hand of your tired father
reaching to switch off the banks of lights,
the rotating gold-and-scalloped Shell sign:
your cue to drag in displays and wiper racks
and start thinking about a bed somewhere.

## Souvenirs

*after William Matthews*

For years, my friend carried in his wallet a tattered receipt
from the Tropicana Motel in Denton, Texas. I gave him
the receipt because keeping it had been a way to wall up
a moment I wanted to remember. A souvenir, the receipt
marked an afternoon with a Texas woman who wanted me,
so I thought, since it was her idea to get the room. It was
1973. Poetry got you laid. Poets were cool. Bob Dylan-
Leonard Cohen cool. It was my 19th birthday, I was still
a virgin. I tried to interest her by reciting a poem aloud.
In the words of William Matthews: *for that was how*
*I thought poetry worked: you digested experience and*
*shat literature.* Matthews was talking 1960, New York,
but I thought it might be true in Texas. True for me, too.
There was a war on. (Isn't there always?) The woman
had shoulder-length red hair and laughed and leaned
forward, breasts and hair spilling. She took a swig
from a long-neck Lone Star, swallowed, and asked
why I wanted her to be my first, as if there was one
right answer to unlock her. I needed help like Bill
Matthews gives on the subject of last words: *Relax.*
*You'll think of something. Let nature take its course.*
I was no Leonard Cohen, no Bob Dylan, but I had
a poem burning a hole in the pocket of a clean shirt.
Fucking Texas. I didn't get laid. I did feel lucky—
lucky not to be in the Republic of South Viet Nam.
To know the names of poets like William Matthews
who, down the road from Denton, I'd get to meet.
I gave my friend the receipt. Said, *I've carried this.*

## Your Cheatin' Heart

My parents sat me down in front of a circular-screen tv.
Shoved a white Tupperware of buttered popcorn in my lap.
And I saw the actor George Hamilton lip-synching Hank Sr.,
singing onstage at the Ryman Auditorium, the Grand Ole Opry.
My parents had spun his records most nights on an RCA turntable.
So what if the sheet music flying by in black-and-white montage
bore the likeness of Hank and not George Hamilton. So what if Elvis
tested for Hank and was rejected by Miss Audrey. And so what if she,
Hank's wife, Miss Audrey, a redhead, was played by a platinum blonde.
Hank Williams sang about a light and dark that he carried, of shared pain,
of the burdensomeness of being poor and alive and just trying to hang on.
The gospel of the heartbreak that happens all the time to ordinary people.
So what if Hank slumped over on the road somewhere in West Virginia.
Died without any memorable last words in the back seat of a Cadillac.
He was on his way to a New Year's Day concert in Canton, Ohio—
we were in Ohio, refugees from the collapse of the price of coal,
he was one of ours, a friend. What's a little morphine sulfate
with a shot of B-12 (and a booze chaser) between friends?

## Atlas of Ohio and Nineteen Ninety

Everywhere we went that summer, the heat had the last word.
But delight is an isotope of knowing to pile into your beater-car
and then take Interstate 71 South past the Mason, Ohio Bob Evans
to King's Island. We parked. Rode the Yogi Bear yellow shuttle.
I paid at a window so that we could pass through the turnstiles
and stand still—they took a picture they said would be waiting
when we returned. I had the hand of the five-year-old, my son,
who wanted to ride everything his ten-year-old brother rode.
I walked with him. Explained height requirements. Glanced
at my wife. On the log run where you get splashed, I rode
behind her. Seated like that—her in front and me behind—
I remembered how love starts and stops and starts again.
In line for the Blue Racer, I took our oldest by the hand.
Passed by a phalanx of pedestal-mount oscillating fans.
The maintenance man with a mermaid tattoo on his arm
smiled at my army. Slapped some pink putty on a crack
running floor to ceiling where riders waited, staring up
at a repair job resembling nothing if not old bubblegum
or the spun-sugar on a paper cone they call cotton candy.
My standing army was two boys, a puzzle of a wife and me.
I was thirty-six, more than a little breathless from life thus far.
A maintenance man had looked at me as if he understood.
And I wanted to let the cool breeze be the years to come
as I listened to my wife explaining gravity, centripetal
and centrifugal forces, as I took a seat in a coaster car
the way my father had before I enlisted in the air force.
At the drop, that smiling-stranger oldest boy of mine
raised his arms. I love recalling how happy we were.
I like to take out the key chain stamped *Kings Island*
and stare into its lighted room at the photograph of us
and consider who I was then and remember the pleasure
of being that man and loved, though love is as inconstant
as currents of air or the radio on any long drive home.

## Suitable for Framing

Because it's his day off, Roy isn't wearing
his brown Shell uniform and ballcap, brown
front-zippered coveralls, but pumps gasoline
and wipes another windshield as if he were.
Numbers spin to a stop as he tops off a tank.
He's wearing a car coat. Black dress slacks.
Leather gloves. Black wing-tip dress shoes.
He thinks about appropriate working attire,
the rules for holding a Shell franchise license,
as he makes smalltalk through an inch or so
of cranked-downed car window. There are
questions about a thieving mechanic named
Delbert Collins who chewed Beeman's Gum.
Lines of flapping, plastic seasonal pennants
snap like sails. He takes a can of motor oil
from a display by the pumps. He gives it
a silver curving spout. Thrusts it, the can
and silver spout, under a raised car hood.
He waits—this Roy, this lucky man—as
the noisy pennants deck the halls of the air.
By a pyramid of snow tires, he counts bills
and Top Value Stamps into a gloved hand—
it's years before self-serve convenience-stores
and still possible to pay yourself a living wage
wiping something, anything, with a shop rag.
Roy can come in on his day off, if he wants to.
Freeze, mid-pivot, in numbing cold as if he's
forgotten a thing he'll remember later, inside.

## Fans Listening to a Boxing Match Over the Radio, June 22, 1938

*"Each time Joe Louis won a fight in those depression years, even before he became champion, thousands of black Americans on relief or WPA, and poor, would throng out into the streets all across the land to march and cheer and yell and cry because of Joe's one-man triumphs. No one else in the United States has ever had such an effect on Negro emotions—or on mine. I marched and cheered and yelled and cried, too."*
—Langston Hughes

A friend from Detroit, Butch Thompson, once said
that being black in America is an art. He said you
practice it the way some paint or learn how to box.
In a photograph at the New York Historical Society
they're listening to the Louis-Schmeling rematch—
a barroom of faces, mostly black men in skimmer hats,
a woman in a Juliet cap, before a portrait of Joe Louis.
An aproned bartender has a hand on the dial of a Philco
cathedral radio as if what most men, some women too,
want between watered drinks is murderous syncopation
for the soundtrack of our curses when peace doesn't cut it.
Joe Louis must have drawn a crowd like someone giving
away what we forgot we wanted. The woman at the bar
is years away from dying of a cerebral hemorrhage or

broken heart or the umpteenth lungful of foul city air.
If there's an art to being black, as Butch said, we see it
in group photographs in rooms like this, the dark gloss
of humanity become a face among other faces. I was
about to say *A happy face* and then caught myself—
see the hatless man, head turned and staring straight
into the camera. That's not the face of a happy man.
In a land of thieves, the usual sawed-off under the bar
isn't there for regulars. It's there because, well, because.
If history has a center, it's here. In a bar in New York
in the nineteen thirties. Ask the staring man, standing
as if aware this is his shot at eternal anything. Ask him
if it's the damage Louis is doing binds them together.
That he's destroying a Nazi poster boy doesn't hurt.

## Us and Them

Sgt. Joe Williams slides off the shrink-wrap packaging.
Unsleeves a Pink Floyd record. *The Dark Side of the Moon.*
Every noon he departs Chanute Air Force Base to drive to
his apartment in Rantoul. To roll a chubby joint. Smoke it.
He's asked me to tag along. Hands me the album jacket,
saying, *I judge a man by how he rolls a joint* and smiling.
When I'm finished, the traffic noise off Illinois 45 is a hum
like Sgt. Joe lighting up, holding smoke and a deep breath.
It isn't easy being enlisted in the spring of '73; the country
detests the war in Vietnam and, by extension, servicemen,
All Things Military—the light-blue short-sleeve shirts
and the darker-blue dress pants, the dress shoes as black
as Henry Kissinger's heart, the US collar brass on blue
garrison caps. Everything about us is the beating drum.
About as popular as Nixon's secret plan to end the war.
The record croons, *You are young and life is long and
there is time to kill today.* This is my first day on base,
first day in the hospital squadron, and I'm baked. Blind.
Trippy rhythms spew through the room, syncing up with
a recorded heartbeat and the sax solo on "Us and Them"
on the altar of stateside service. We do this, not the dying
or being blown apart / pieced together / sent home again—
not the coming home fractured by what light has shown
as true and must then follow you for as long as you live.
Like the burned kids on a road in the famous photograph
where the caption reads "Phan Thi Kim Phuc (center) flees
with other children after South Vietnamese planes mistakenly
dropped napalm on South Vietnamese troops and civilians."
And now I send the air out of my lungs, dreaming of women
as the two of us wait for the country to come to its senses.
To draw deep breaths of Conscience if not moral clarity.
Like the song says, *After all we're only ordinary men.*

## White-Bearded Walt Whitman, Hatted and Holding a Cane

The cane is an accessible weapon he may need, given a violent world
whose wounds he once dressed in the wards of Civil War casualties.
From the entirety that has preceded Matthew Brady's attentiveness,
he is culling a quiet acceptance of whatever's next, including death.
His captain is departed. Embalmed. Celebrated. The tomb pilfered.
He looks out at the lens with the eyes of one who's loved and lost.
Relaxes into the static moment that lies a life is more of the same.
The hand not holding the cane, the right, he buries in a coat pocket.
A chain across a suit vest says he has a timepiece, can announce
an hour and minute; though not with any rejoicing or expectation
that the next appointment, if there is one, will produce any feeling
of triumph after long trial. Make your record, he seems to be saying.
America is the same whore drunk on the gratuity of another sailor.
Leave me to my struggles to find a better word for faithlessness.

## Umbrella

It's, you know, that true love thing.
Divorced but friends. Still pretty tight.

So just fine with being here with me.
At the office of a urologist in Ohio.

If she has a "tell" (that she loves me),
this morning it's her looking away

before the needle enters my penis,
a needle preamble to an anesthetic

if the health care worker fitting you
is skilled. This nurse knows her stuff.

Knows about male pride and a penis
turtling. And laughs, wisecracking

there are times that you just want
to hide from the goddamn world.

The fact a loved one looks away
is a small mercy. An act of grace

that includes being so distracted
by my suffering she leaves behind

a black, folding umbrella that had
saved us from a late-spring rain.

## The Night Boat Tour, 2007

Animatronic lawn reindeer and sleigh translate,
anywhere in Florida, to the new resident missing

the North and snow. We stop at a seafood place
where pelicans scour the dock for French fries,

plundered onion rings their Christmas banquet.
Anyway, I see signage for the night boat tour.

And one of us pays the fare. We climb aboard,
newly rootless, Americans afoot in the world—

judging by large Tomahawk Nation tattoos,
the tour guide must be an FSU fan or alumnus.

Engines engage, thrum noticeably. Under stars.
I don't know about you, love, but I felt something

not unlike the Christ child, freshly manger-dropped—
dare I use the word *happy*—when the boat's wake

turned under and executed a Christmas-tree shape
offshore from groves and live oaks. Pastureland.

## Petaling

The shell-like way of opening the night pulls off
has a name so we won't overlook its onion nature:
petaling. The Air Force was about to spit me out.

A little because I wouldn't shut up about the War,
a little because I was twenty and proud. Mouthy.
I was smoking a joint in August in the Midwest,

standing on the top step of one of the fire escapes
for the Air Force barracks I lived in in those days.
A ledge of wood, an iron ladder for a handhold—

I looked out over the business glow of Rantoul,
northward across blueblack acres of corn field.
That night, the dark had a mouth and practiced

a geophagia as it wolfed down eastern Illinois:
grain elevators and running-horse weathervanes,
the gray sentinel trees in the direction of Chicago.

I wanted nineteen seventy-four swallowed whole.
Nixon, his dour lieutenants and black operatives,
deceptions they used like a smoke to still the hive.

I recall the president was on the verge of resigning,
stepping onto Marine One and ascending like a god,
if by a god you mean a sonofabitch in a suit and tie.

Time on the fire escape was a clock-tick of peace,
if by peace you mean to the south, by a drive-in,
someone was burning tires and that smoke rose.

## Whatever Small Form of Joy Likeness Equals

> *Sometimes a thing can seem star-like*
> *when it's just a star, stripped of whatever small form of joy*
> *likeness equals.*

—Carl Phillips, "Stray"

If displays of affection could light up lives,
a bioluminescence, then what I witnessed as
tenderness in the aisles at a Kroger this evening

should have lit up sizable portions of central Ohio
if not the whole of the Northern Hemisphere—
the couple with garrulous offspring brushed

hands in Produce as something like sparks
flew for a sad 60-something pushed along
in her not-quite-handicapped shopping cart.

Not to mention, those separated by geography
or shared failure lingering in Pizza & Desserts
then by the cold light of the milk and butter aisle,

unsayable and indecent truths resplendent in carton
after carton of eggs that are not the estivation of hope.
Which is what I thought, buying tuna to feed my share

of the winter-exhausted feral cats in the neighborhood:
that kindness begets kindness. And hope. Instant karma.
I bought a case of small cans. Went home and forked

the piscine contents onto plates at the western edge
of the unglaciated Appalachian Plateau. Not hope
or faith or love exactly but what I could manage.

# One Dead, One Among the Living Dead in an Asylum

*from a story told to me by my grandmother, Susan Bentley*

When people or things vanish at Eastern State Hospital,
it invites comparisons to sleight of hand. Prestidigitation.
Something palmed or taken away, and not by angels.
Comfort Rage, my friend, was visiting from her wing.
The Colored Only Wing. She started coughing—
she was a lunger, and sick, but I thought her cough
a tubercular spasm like others she had every so often.
I waited. I was sure she'd start in breathing again.
But when she didn't, I went and found Eugene.
Eugene is what we call the Floorwalker. Someone

who watches over us. He switched on the overhead.
It hummed a small, pure version of the Song of Light.
Eugene stood over Comfort Rage and raised her wrist.
Said, She's gone. And the fluorescents flashed. Winked.
Like a shock had passed through the whining white tubes.
Like what we convert to after this hard life, is electricity.
Comfort would have said believing that wasn't crazy.
Like a fairy god mother, she'd show up if I wished.
Sundays, mostly. She would call out *Susan Bentley!*
I'd stop swaying. Traveling in my mind like I do.

In no time at all, they made sure she was "seen to"—
meaning a pair of colored men came with a stretcher.
To my bed. And lifted the top sheet with her in it.
The men carrying the stretcher were quiet. I knew
not to speak about that, the men being quiet, though
the undeclared swirls up and floats away like smoke.
Truth is, patients at Eastern know not to tell things.
Crazy things. This everyone knows. Like I know
when Comfort Rage left her body—*vanished*—
in the Whites Only Wing, lights flickered.

## Ghosts at the Feast

In a country of the dead there are flocks of phantasmal birds.
The sleek bodies take the air. The air is cologned with going.

Squads of sleepwalkers shuffle under sky droughted of stars.
They pass cedar trees metastasizing into diaphanous moonset.

The architecture is the old, though minus brokenness of spirit
and the tyranny of the straight line. One of several entrances

opens onto an atrium of upholstered seats. A tour is starting.
Schedules are a part of what is revealed and what is hidden.

Black paths flip like flash cards. Some hold up Bic lighters,
the glow an aerial photo of what we expect of the afterlife:

what it was like—the battles to last the night—magnified;
lots of cravings become everlasting and so unanswerable.

Soul is talkative. Here, voices are a gauze the same shade
as last light. My father is there. In the dim with the others.

He whips out a Zippo. Flicks. Again. It sparks. Flames.
A long moment of sun he summons is his parentheses.

Some of the dead travel with ease in the available light.
Most find places at a table having failed to recall why.

Soon, you think, the reason for all this will sink in.
If you're patient, dismissing ideas like Destination.

# Acknowledgments

Poems from *Walking With Eve in the Loved City* are copyright © 2018 by The University of Arkansas Press. Reprinted with the permission of The Permissions Company, LLC on behalf of publisher, www.uapress.com. These poems, specifically: "Robert Plant Holding a Dove that Flew into His Hands, Circa 1973"; "Our Local Heavens"; "How Not to Spell *Gymnasium;* 1975"; "Walking with Eve in the Loved City"; "Jeff Goldblum in *The Fly*"; "Fitzgerald and Zelda, February 1921"; "Saturday Afternoon at The Midland Theatre in Newark, Ohio"; "Whatever Else, This Memory Resembles a Dance"; "The Silence of the Belt When It Is Not Striking the Child"; "Can't Help Falling in Love"; "The Force of Right Words"; "Ringo Starr Answers Questions on *Larry King Live* about the Death of George Harrison"; "The Dark Knight, On His Day Off"; "Hellhound"; "Transcendence"; "Woman and Alligator"; "Nosferatu in Florida"; "Unicyclist with UM Umbrella"; "Watching the Night Approach of Tropical Storm Rita"; "Dixie Highway"; "At the Wheel of the *Pilar,* Ernest Hemingway Addresses the Breezes off the Coast of Cuba"; "Live Nudes; Jim Morrison & The Doors in Miami, 1969"; "Rimbaud Dying"; "The Nascent Soul Selects a Set of Appalachian Parents"; and "Lee in the Orchard, 1865." (Thanks, always, to Billy Collins.)

My thanks to the editors of the magazines in which the new poems first appeared:

*Adirondack Review,* "American Landscape with Boys in a Car"
*American Athenaeum,* "Wild Monkeys to Measure Radiation Levels in Fukushima"
*Cactus Heart,* "Texas History"
*Cumberland River Review,* "My Mother's Red Ford"
*The Florida Review,* "Rebel Rebel"
*Free State Review,* "Dream Caused by the Flight of a Bee around a Pomegranate a Second before Awakening" and "Approaching Seattle"
*Gargoyle,* "The Spell for Stopping Those Who Take Everything"
*The Magnolia Review,* "Whatever Small Form of Joy Likeness Equals"
*New Works Review,* "Four-torch Juggling"
*One,* "Oahu Theory"
*Orange Coast Review,* "Lost Storyline from *The Life of the Flying Man*"
*Oxford Magazine,* "Fans Listening to a Boxing Match Over the Radio, June 22, 1938"
*Poydras Review,* "Atlas of Ohio and Nineteen Ninety"
*Red Savina Review,* "He Spent a Year Hallucinating Peace"
*Solstice Literary Review,* "Whole Lotta Shakin' Goin' On"
*Steinbeck Now,* "Your Cheatin' Heart" and "Minuteman Missile"
*Still: The Journal,* "The Night Boat Tour, 2007"
*Tipton Poetry Journal,* "One Dead, One Among the Living Dead in an Asylum"
*What Rough Beast,* "Umbrella"
*Wilderness House Literary Review,* "The Leaping Cat's Human Assistant".

My sincere thanks to the National Endowment for the Arts, the Ohio Arts Council, and the Florida Division of Cultural Affairs for fellowships awarded during the writing of this book.

"This Is Not a Dark Ride" and "Radio Nowhere" appeared in *Love Poems & Other Messages for Bruce Springsteen* published by Pudding House Publications in 2009.

"Spirit Recordings" first appeared in the chapbook *The Idiot's Guide to the Afterlife* published by Pudding House Books.

"Fans Listening to a Boxing Match Over the Radio, June 22, 1938" won the Golden Ox Award for poetry for work published in *Oxford Magazine* in 2016.

"The Nascent Soul Selects a Set of Appalachian Parents" was a *Today's Poem* selection on *Poetry Daily* on April 27, 2019.